LET'S TALK
CANTONESE

Victoria Liu
Joseph Durra

JBD Language Series
JBD Publishing, Inc. • San Francisco-USA

LET'S TALK CANTONESE

Published by JBD Publishing, Inc.
400 Pacific Avenue
San Francisco, California 94133, USA

First edition 1994

Cover Design:
Collaboration, Inc., San Francisco

Book Layout Design:
UniTex DTP Express Service, Oakland
Collaboration, Inc., San Francisco

Typesetting:
UniTex DTP Express Service, Oakland

Audio Production:
JBD Productions

Printed in the United States of America

ISBN: 1-8811906-03-5

TABLE OF CONTENTS

PREFACE

Welcome to **LET'S TALK CANTONESE** !

You are about to embark on an adventure - learning a new language. The **LET'S TALK** method makes it easy for you to learn because we teach you to converse in Cantonese the same way you first learned your native language as a child. By building on words, phrases and then sentences you learn to speak naturally.

We have limited the traditional vocabulary and grammar drills because drills do not teach you to converse just as playing piano scales does not teach you to play melodies. All languages are made up of three parts - pronunciation, vocabulary and grammar. You should keep this simple fact in mind as you proceed.

The **LET'S TALK** method teaches you vocabulary and grammar at the same time by teaching you sentences pertaining to everyday life. The teaching is so subtle that you are not conscious of learning vocabulary and grammar as such. Of course, we do give you grammar notes and vocabulary lists because adult learners, in particular, like to have reasons for things.

Pronunciation is taught by learning the phonetic system we use called the Yale System. The audio tapes are valuable listening tools as the words are pronounced by native speakers. There are pauses in the tape which allow you to pronounce the words and compare your pronunciation with the native speaker. Constant playing of these tapes at home or in your car will familiarize you with correct pronunciation.

LET'S TALK CANTONESE

A few words about the Cantonese language itself. Do not be intimidated because the sound of the language is so much different from English. Hearing and speaking the first few Cantonese words will remove your fears and gradually the language will become familiar. Do not let the tones discourage you. We'll let you in on a secret. Even if you get the tone wrong you will probably be understood! People hear meaning through context. Even in conversing in English, a listener retains only a small portion of what you say, but he or she understands what you said. So with tones.

We have a chart to illustrate tones and you will find that basically there are two tones (rising and falling) that need to be learned. Vowel sounds have been arranged so that 10 will do the job instead of the 51 in most textbooks.

All the dialogues have been updated to today's usage and we give you a number of supplementary expressions for emergencies and other needs. Remember that when you speak just a few words to a Cantonese native, you will get a smile of surprise because of the rarity of Westerners speaking Cantonese. The smile will bring warmth and both you and the listener will feel good about communicating even on a basic level. Communication is what language learning is all about.

Producing this program has been a real challenge as we have created an entirely new method for language learning - a method designed to make learning rewarding and effective. You will acquire early on a sense of satisfaction which will give you the enthusiasm to continue.

The Authors

INTRODUCTION

LET'S TALK CANTONESE is a specifically designed audio course for teaching English speakers conversational Cantonese quickly and easily. It is ideal for business people and language students as a self-taught course. The textbook can be used for conversation classes.

The course consists of four one-hour audio tapes and a textbook: LEVEL 1 with 13 basic lessons, LEVEL 2 with 23 dialogues and a tri-lingual glossary. Both levels contain 800 items of vocabulary and expressions made up from about 2000 basic Cantonese words. Basic grammar is taught through dialogues arranged in 30 contemporary topics. The course takes the learner from beginning to low intermediate level.

ARRANGEMENT OF THE COURSE

LEVEL 1 : 13 basic lessons

We begin by teaching words and expressions in simple, interactive sentences with English translations. The learner is given the opportunity to acquire pronunciation as well as communication skills at the survival level with such topics as introductions, family, job, food and drink, numbers, time, money, and prices. We eliminate vocabulary lists and grammar notes in LEVEL 1 because we use a short cut: learning to speak by speaking whole sentences.

LEVEL 2: 23 Dialogues

The following format is used for each unit:

1. **Dialogue**

2. **Vocabulary**

3. **Sentence Patterns**

4. **Brief Grammar Notes**

5. **Translation of the Dialogue**

Note: Following the dialogues we have provided translations in Cantonese for those who can read Cantonese characters and for English speakers to get assistance from Cantonese speaking friends.

All the basic lessons and dialogues are bilingual using Yale system phonetics and English. Four audio cassettes accompany the textbook.

HOW TO USE THE COURSE

To get the best results from the course:

1. Skim the lesson or the dialogue in English to see what you are going to learn.

2. Listen to the lesson or the dialogue tape and repeat again and again with the book shut. Go through paragraph by paragraph. Don't try to learn too many sentences at one time.

3. Listen to the vocabulary tape and respond to the English translation to refresh your memory. Make sure that you memorize all new words before you go on to the next lesson.

4. Read the grammar notes of each lesson to learn the rules and try to remember the key sentence patterns.

5. Reviewing and using the language is the most important step. Find a partner to do role play or practice with native Cantonese speakers.

A few notes on how we handle the boring stuff of language learning:

1. Drills

We have eliminated the traditional mechanical pattern drills, but have cleverly put them into the dialogues, which is a more practical and interesting way to learn. You will remember sentences and vocabulary much better using the dialogues.

2. Grammar

Grammar rules are generally the most frustrating and difficult things to learn and apply to practical conversation. Our philosophy about rules of grammar is that less is more at the beginning and low intermediate stage.

LET'S TALK CANTONESE

You will note that we explain some rules in the grammar notes sections of the book. These rules are generalized and written in simple language to aid the learner and they are reviewed and reused in the dialogues. There are exceptions to some of these rules, but you will learn them as you speak and get corrected by a kindly Cantonese speaker. Clutter is bad for learning.

The *LET'S TALK* method was first devised to teach English. We have two programs for teaching English - beginning/intermediate and advanced. These programs use videotape as the teaching medium and are sold in the U.S., Canada, Hong Kong and mainland China. So the method has been proved by thousands of satisfied learners.

We are certain you will find, as thousands have, that *LET'S TALK CANTONESE*, like other *LET'S TALK* programs, teaches you in a unique way that engages and motivates. Good luck!

INTRODUCTION TO PRONUNCIATION OF CANTONESE

The system for Cantonese pronunciation used in this book is the Yale system. Cantonese words are usually composed of one or two syllables made up of the following three elements:

1. Initials. A beginning consonant called an initial, i.e. fā.

2. Finals. A final is either a vowel (fā) or a vowel with a consonant (baat).

3. Tones. While there are a total of seven tones in Cantonese, they can be reduced to three: rising, falling and level. The other four tones are variations in pitch of the three main tones, i.e. a high (rising) tone, a low (rising) tone, and an even tone. Do not be intimidated by this - you will understand it by listening to the tapes.

The tones are indicated by the use of diacritical marks over the first vowel in the word. The letter "h" after the last vowel in the word indicates a low tone.

	FALLING	RISING	LEVEL
High	sì （施）	sí （史）	sī （絲）
Mid			si （試）
Low	sìh （時）	síh （市）	sih （事）

Note: High level and high falling tones are virtually indistinguishable. In Sidney Lau's system (Hong Kong), these two tones have been combined.

The 19 Cantonese Initials (Consonants)

SYMBOL	PRONOUNCED AS IN:	EXAMPLE IN CANTONESE	MEANING IN ENGLISH
B	Boy	baat	eight
D	Dad	dá	beat
Ch	Chair	chéng	invite
F	Five	fā	flower
G	Guy	gāai	street
Gw	Guava	gwai	expensive
H	Hot	hā	shrimp
J	Jaw	jó	left
K	Key	kāt	cough
Kw	Quart	kwàhn	skirt
L	Low	lóuh	old
M	Mama	máh	horse
N	Nail	néih	you
Ng	Wing	ngóh	I
P	Pair	pèhng	inexpensive
S	See	sī	poem
T	Toy	tói	table
W	Want	wán	look for
Y	Yowl	yáuh	have

10 Cantonese Vowel Sounds

	Yale	IPA	Pronounced as in:		Yale	IPA	Pronounced as in:
1	A	[a]	m<u>a</u>ma	6	I	[I]	l<u>i</u>ve
2	Aa	[a:]	d<u>ah</u>	7	iu	[iu]	y<u>ie</u>ld
3	E	[e]	b<u>e</u>d	8	O	[ɔ]	b<u>o</u>ss
4	Ei	[ei]	d<u>ay</u>	9	Oo	[u:]	c<u>oo</u>l
5	Eu	[ə:]	n<u>u</u>rse	10	U	[u]	b<u>oo</u>k

The 10 vowels above are the basic vowel sounds. When one or two of these vowels are combined with the Initials (consonants), they form the Yale System Cantonese Finals illustrated below for reference. All you need to learn are these 10 vowels.

51 Cantonese Finals (B)

A [a] as in m<u>a</u>ma		
Yale	**Key Word**	**English meaning**
A	F<u>ā</u>	flower
Ai	S<u>ai</u>	small
Au	G<u>au</u>	enough
Am	S<u>àm</u>	heart
An	M<u>ān</u>	dollar
Ang	D<u>áng</u>	wait
Ap	S<u>ah</u>p	ten
At	Ch<u>āt</u>	seven
Ak	Ch<u>e</u>k	ruler

Aa [a:] as in d<u>a</u>h		
Yale	**Key Word**	**English meaning**
Aai	D<u>aai</u>	put on
Aau	G<u>aau</u>	teach
Aam	Sà<u>am</u>	three
Aan	D<u>áan</u>	bill
Aang	H<u>āang</u>	pit
Aap	Ng<u>aap</u>	duck
Aat	B<u>aat</u>	eight
Aak	H<u>āak</u>	black

I [i] as in l<u>i</u>ve Iu [iu] as in y<u>ie</u>ld		
Yale	**Key Word**	**English meaning**
I	S<u>i</u>	try
Iu	S<u>íu</u>	small
Im	G<u>im</u>	sword
In	T<u>ì</u>n	sky
Ing	S<u>ing</u>	last name
Ip	Y<u>ihp</u>	leaf
It	Y<u>iht</u>	hot
Ik	S<u>ihk</u>	eat

O [ɔ] as in b<u>o</u>ss		
Yale	**Key Word**	**English meaning**
O	Ng<u>ó</u>h	I
Oi	H<u>òi</u>	open
Ou	G<u>òu</u>	tall
On	G<u>òn</u>	dry
Ong	F<u>óng</u>	room
Ot	H<u>ot</u>	thirsty
Ok	Gw<u>ok</u>	country

E [e] as in b<u>e</u>d		
Yale	**Key Word**	**English Meaning**
E	Chè	car
Ei	Bé<u>i</u>	give
Ek	T<u>ek</u>	kick
Eng	L<u>eng</u>	pretty
Eu	Hè<u>u</u>	boots
Eui	Sé<u>ui</u>	water
Euk	G<u>euk</u>	foot
Eun	S<u>eun</u>	letter
Eung	Sé<u>ung</u>	want to
Eut	Ch<u>ēut</u>	out

U [u] as in b<u>oo</u>k		
Yale	**Key Word**	**English Meaning**
U	G<u>ú</u>	guess
Ui	W<u>úi</u>	meeting
Un	W<u>ún</u>	bowl
Uk	S<u>ūk</u>	uncle
Ut	F<u>ut</u>	wide
Ung	S<u>ung</u>	give

Y		
Yale	**Key Word**	**English Meaning**
Yu	Sy<u>ù</u>	book
Yun	Sy<u>ùn</u>	sour
Yut	Sy<u>ut</u>	snow

LET'S TALK CANTONESE

LEVEL 1

BASIC LESSONS

Haih, Ǹ haih, Haih Ǹ haih?

To be, not to be, to be?

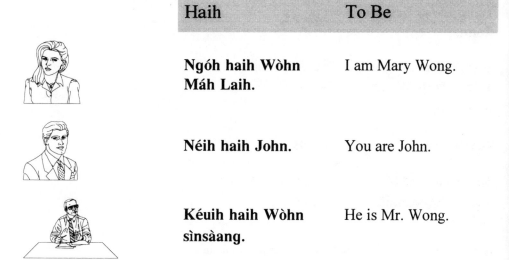

Haih	To Be
Ngóh haih Wòhn Máh Laih.	I am Mary Wong.
Néih haih John.	You are John.
Kéuih haih Wòhn sìnsàang.	He is Mr. Wong.

Ngóh - Ngóh - Ngóh	I - I - I
Néih - Néih - Néih	You - You - You
Kéuih - Kéuih - Kéuih	He - He - He / She - She - She

M̀ haih	Not to Be

Ngóh m̀haih John. Ngóh haih Máh Laih.
I am not John. I am Mary.

Néih m̀haih Máh Laih. Néih haih John.
You are not Mary. You are John.

Kéuih m̀haih John. Kéuih haih Wòhn Sìnsàang.
He is not John. He is Mr. Wong.

Haih	To Be

Ngóh haih Máh Laih. Ngóh haih beisyù.
I am Mary. I am a secretary.

Note: The word for "*you*" - **néih** - is frequently pronounced as "*léih*". "*I*" - **ngóh** - is sometimes pronounced as "*óh*".

Néih haih John. Néih haih sèungyàhn.	You are John. You are a businessman.
Kéuih haih Wòhn sìnsàang. Wòhn sìnsàang haih bōsí.	He is Mr. Wong. Mr. Wong is a boss. 
Ngóh - Néih - Kéuih	I - You - He (She)
Ngóhge - Néihge - Kéuihge	My - Your - His (Her)

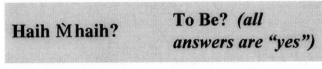

Haih M̀ haih?	**To Be?** *(all answers are "yes")*

Néih haih m̀haih John?	Are you John?
Haih, ngóh haih John.	Yes, I am John. 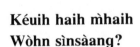
Kéuih haih m̀haih Wòhn sìnsàang?	Is he Mr. Wong?
Haih, kéuih haih Wòhn sìnsàang.	Yes, he is Mr. Wong. 

LET'S TALK CANTONESE

| Ngóh haih m̀haih Máh Laih? | Am I Mary? |
| Haih, néih haih Máh Laih. | Yes, you are Mary. |

| **Haih M̀ haih?** | **To Be?** *(all answers are no)* |

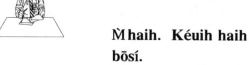

John haih m̀haih bōsí?	Is John a boss?
M̀ haih. Kéuih haih sèungyàhn.	No. John is a businessman.
Wòhn sìnsàang haih m̀haih beisyù?	Is Mr. Wong a secretary?

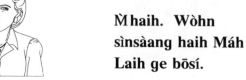

| M̀ haih. Kéuih haih bōsí. | No. Mr. Wong is a boss. |
| Wòhn sìnsàang haih m̀haih néihge bōsí? | Is Mr. Wong your boss? |

| M̀ haih. Wòhn sìnsàang haih Máh Laih ge bōsí. | No. Mr. Wong is Mary's boss. |

Ngóhge - Néihge - Kéuihge - Máh Laih ge

My - Your - His - Mary's

Bīnwái? Bīngo?

Who?

Néih haih bīnwái?	Who are you?
Ngóh haih John.	I am John.
Ngóh sing Léih.	My last name is Lee.
Kéuih haih bīnwái?	Who is he?
Kéuih haih Daaih Mìhng.	He is Da Ming.
Kéuih sing Chàhn.	His last name is Chang.

Kéuih haih bīnwái?	Who is she?
Kéuih haih John ge taaitáai.	She is John's wife.

Kéuih sing Hòh.	Her last name is Ho.
Bīngo haih néih sìnsàang?	Who is your husband?
Kéuih haih ngóh sìnsàang.	He is my husband.

Kéuih sing Jèung.	His last name is Cheung.
Bīngo haih néihge bōsí?	Who is your boss?
Kéuih haih ngóhge bōsí.	He is my boss.

Kéuih sing Wòhn.	His last name is Wong.
Bīngo haih néihge beisyù?	Who is your secretary?

Máh Laih haih ngóhge beisyù. Mary is my secretary.

Kéuih sing Làuh. Her last name is Lau.

Chàhn - Léih - Jeung - Wòhn - Hòh - Làuh Chang - Lee - Cheung - Wong - Ho - Lau

Nīgo haih ____.

This is ____.

Kéuihdeih haih bīnwái?	Who are they?
Nīgo haih ngóh bàhbā.	This is my father.
Nīgo haih ngóh màhmā.	This is my mother.
Nīgo haih ngóh gājē.	This is my elder sister.

Nīgo haih ngóh agō. This is my elder brother.

Yáuh *tùhng* Móuh

To Have and *Don't have*

Nīgo haih m̀haih néih mùihmúi?	Is this your younger sister?
M̀haih. Kéuih haih ngóhge pàhngyáuh.	No, she is not. She is my friend.
Ngóh móuh mùihmúi.	I don't have a younger sister.
Nīgo haih m̀haih néih dàihdái?	Is this your younger brother?

M̀ haih. Kéuih haih ngóhge pàhngyáuh.	No, he is my friend.
Ngóh móuh dàihdái.	I don't have a younger brother.
Néih yáuh bàhbā, màhmā, agō, tùhng gājē.	You have a father, a mother, an elder brother, and an elder sister.
Daahnhaih neih móuh dàihdái tùhng mùihmúi.	But you don't have a younger brother and a younger sister.
Néih nē?	How about you?
Ngóh móuh báhbā, máhmā.	I don't have a father or a mother.
Ngóh yáuh agō, gājē, dàihdái túhng mùihmúi.	I have an elder brother, an elder sister, a younger brother and a younger sister.

Dihnghaih . . .?

Or...?

| **Néih haih John dihnghaih Wòhn sìnsàang?** | Are you John or Mr. Wong? |

| **Ngóh haih John.** | I am John. |

| **Néih haih sèungyàhn dihnghaih beisyù?** | Are you a businessman or a secretary? |

| **Ngóh haih beisyù.** | I am a secretary. |

Wòhn sìnsàang haih néihge bōsí dihnghaih Máh Laih ge bōsí?	Is Mr. Wong your boss or mary's boss?	
Wòhn sìnsàang haih Máh Laih ge bōsí.	Mr. Wong is Mary's boss.	
Máh Laih haih néihge beisyù dihnghaih kéuihge beisyù?	Is Mary your secretary or his secretary?	
Máh Laih haih kéuihge beisyù.	Mary is his secretary.	

Yáuh Móuh ____?

Do you have ____?

Néih yáuh móuh jáinéui?	Do you have children?
Móuh. Ngóh meih gitfān.	No. I am not married.
Néih yáuh móuh nàahm pàhngyáuh?	Do you have a boyfriend?
Yáuh, nīgo haih ngóh nàahm pàhngyáuh. Kéuih haih leuhtsī.	Yes, this is my boyfriend. He is a lawyer.
Néih yáuh móuh taaitáai?	Do you have a wife?
Móuh. Ngóh meih gitfān.	No. I 'm not married.

Néih yáuh móuh néuih pàhngyáuh?   Do you have a girlfriend?

Yáuh, nīgo haih ngóh néuih pàhngyáuh. Kéuih haih wuihgai.   Yes, this is my girlfriend. She is an accountant.

Nīdī haih mātyéh?
What is this?

Mātyéh?	What?
Nīdī haih mātyéh?	What is this?
Nīdī haih chàh.	This is tea.
Gódī haih mātyéh?	What is that?
Gódī haih gafē.	That is coffee.

Nīdī haih mātyéh? — What is this?

Nīdī haih Hóháu-hólohk. — This is Coca-Cola.

Gódī haih mātyéh? — What is that?

Gódī haih Chàthéi. — That is 7-Up.

Dihnghaih . . .? Or . . .?

Nīdī haih Hóháu-hólohk dihnghaih Chàthéi? — Is this Coca-Cola or 7-Up?

Nīdī haih Chàthéi. — This is 7-Up.

Nīdī haih mātyéh? — What is this?

Nīdī haih mihnbāau. — This is bread.

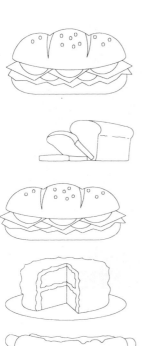

Gódī haih mātyéh?	What is that?
Gódī haih sàammàhnjih.	That's a sandwich.
Nīdī haih mihnbāau dihnghaih sàammàhnjih?	Is this bread or a sandwich?
Nīdī haih sàammàhnjih.	This is a sandwich.
Nīdī haih mātyéh?	What is this?
Nīdī haih daahngòu.	This is cake.
Gódī haih mātyéh?	What is that?
Gódī haih yihtgáu.	That is a hot dog.
Nīdī haih daahngòu dihnghaih yihtgáu?	Is this cake or a hot dog?
Nīdī haih yihtgáu.	This is a hot dog.

Haih m̀haih . . .?   Is this . . .?

Nīdī haih m̀haih Hóháu-hólohk?	Is this Coca-Cola?	
M̀haih. Nīdī haih chàh. Nīdī haih mātyéh?	No. It's tea. What is this?	
Chàthéi. Gódī haih chàh dihnghaih gafē?	7-Up. Is that tea or coffee?	
Gafē. Néih yáuh móuh Hóháu-hólohk?	Coffee. Do you have Coca-Cola?	
Yáuh. Nàh. Néih yáuh móuh mihnbāau?	Yes. Here it is. Do you have bread?	
Yáuh. Nàh.	Yes. Here it is.	

Jùng m̀jùngyi ＿＿＿?
(Jùngyi/M̀ jùngyi)
Do you like＿＿?(Like/Don't like)

Ngóh jùngyi Hóháu-hólohk. Ngóh m̀jùngyi Chàthéi.

I like Coca-Cola. I don't like 7-Up.

Ngóh jùngyi gafē. Ngóh m̀jùngyi chàh.

I like coffee. I don't like tea.

Néih jùng m̀jùngyi Hóháu-hólohk?

Do you like Coca-Cola?

M̀ jùngyi. Ngóh jùngyi Chàthéi. Néih jùng m̀jùngyi gafē?

No, I don't. I like 7-Up. Do you like coffee?

23

Ṁjùngyi. Ngóh jùngyi chàh.	No, I don't. I like tea.

* * * * * * * * * *

Ngóh jùngyi pìhnggwó. Ngóh ṁjùngyi cháang.	I like apples. I don't like oranges.

Ngóh jùngyi sihdòbèiléi. Ngóh ṁjùngyi tóu.	I like strawberries. I don't like peaches.

Néih jùng ṁjùngyi pìhnggwó?	Do you like apples?

Ṁjùngyi. Ngóh jùngyi cháang. Néih jùng ṁjùngyi sihdòbèiléi?	No, I don't. I like oranges. Do you like strawberries?

Ṁjùngyi. Ngóh jùngyi tóu.	No, I don't. I like peaches.

* * * * * * * * * *

Ngóh yáuh pìhnggwó tùhng cháang. Néih yiu mātyéh?

I have apples and oranges. What would you like?

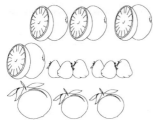

Ngóh yiu cháang. Ngóh jùngyi cháang. Ngóh yáuh sihdòbèiléi tùhng tóu. Néih yiu mātyéh?

I would like an orange. I like oranges. I have strawberries and peaches. What would you like?

Ngóh yiu tóu. Ngóh jungyi tóu.

I would like a peach. I like peaches.

* * * * *

* * * * *

Ngóh yáuh Hóháu- hólohk tùhng Chàthéi. Néih yiu mātyéh?

I have Coca-Cola and 7-Up. What would you like?

Ngóh yiu Chàthéi. Ngóh yáuh gafē tùhng chàh. Néih yiu mātyéh?

I would like a 7-Up. I have coffee and tea. What would you like?

Ngóh yiu chàh. M̀ gòi.

I would like tea. Thank you.

UNIT 9

Soumuhk
Numbers

A. 1-10	B. 11-19
1 - yāt	*sahp + (1-9)*
2 - yih	11 - sahp yāt
3 - sàam	12 - sahp yih
4 - sei	13 - sahp sàam
5 - nǵh	.
6 - luhk	.
7 - chāt	19 - sahp gáu
8 - baat	
9 - gáu	
10 - sahp	

C. 20, 30, 40 etc.	D. 21-99

(2-9) + sahp

20 - yih sahp

30 - sàam sahp

40 - sei sahp

.

.

90 gáu sahp

(1-9) + sahp + (1-9)

21 - yih sahp yāt

32 - sàam sahp yih

43 - sei sahp sàam

.

.

99 gáu sahp gáu

Yìhgā Géidím?

What time is it?

Yìhgā Géidím?	What time is it?
Léuhng dím.	2:00

Chāt dím.	7:00

Yāt dím bun.	1:30

Sei dím . 4:00

Sahp yāt dím ngh sahp ngh fàn. 11:55

a) **Sahp dím ngh.** 10:25
b) **Sahp dím yih sahp ngh fàn.**

Sahp dím sahp sàam fàn. 10:13

Ngh dím chāt. 5:35

Gáu dím lìhng sàam fàn. 9:03

Sàam dím.   3:00

Gáu dím.   9:00

a) **Sahp dím léuhng.**   10:10
b) **Sahp dím sahp fàn.**

Sahp yih dím.   12:00

a) **Sahp yih dím ńgh.**   12:25
b) **Sahp yih dím yih sahp ńgh fàn.**

Chín tùhng Fobaih
Money and Currency

	in Hong Kong	in Canton, China
one penny/cent	**yāt go sīn**	**yāt fān chìhn**
ten cents	**yāt hòuhjí**	**yāt hòuhjí**
one dollar	**yāt mān**	**yāt mān**
coins	**sáanngán**	**ngánjái**
one dollar bill	**yāt mān jí**	**yāt mān jí**

Hong Kong currency	**Gónjí**
	Góngbaih
	Góngngán
Chinese currency	**Yàhnmàhnbaih**
US Currency	**Méihgām**
	Méihyùhn

UNIT 12

Máaih Dím Sàam
Tùhng Nǵh Chāan
Ordering Dim-Sum and Lunch

M̀goi, ngóh yiu yāt go chàsìubàau.	Excuse me, I'd like a steamed barbecued pork bun.
M̀goi, ngóh yiu yāt lùhng hàgáau.	Excuse me, I'd like an order of steamed shrimp dumplings.
M̀goi, ngóh yiu yāt lùhng sìumáai tùhng yāt go daahntāat.	Excuse me, I'd like an order of steamed dumplings and one egg-custard.
M̀goi, ngóh yiu yāt go cháau mihn.	Excuse me, I'd like an order of fried noodles.

Ṁgòi, ngóh yiu yāt diph cháau faahn tùhng yāt wún wàhntàn mihn.

Excuse me, I'd like an order of fried rice and a bowl of won-ton noodles.

Ṁgòi, ngóh yiu sei go wòtip tùhng yāt būi luhk chàh.

Excuse me, I'd like four potstickers and a cup of green tea.

UNIT 13

Mahnhauh, Dòjeh tùhng Sàn Nìhn Jūk Yuhn

Greetings, New Year's Wishes, and Thank you

1. **Néih hóu ma?**   How are you?
   Géi hóu, yáuhsàm.   Fine, thank you.
   Néih nē?   And how about you?
   Màhmádéi.   So-so.

2. **Jóusàhn!**   Good morning!

3. **Jóutáu!**   Good night!

4. **Joigin!**   Good-bye.
   Bāaibaai!   Bye-bye.

5. **Dòjeh!**   Thank you (for gift).
   M̀ sái haakhei!   You're welcome.

6. **Ṁgòi!** — Thank you (for service).
   Ṁsáiṁgòi! — You are welcome.

7. **Ṁgòisaai!** — Thank you very much.

8. **Deuiṁjyuh!** — Sorry.
   Ṁgán yiu! — That's okay.

9. **Ṁhóuyisi!** — Sorry (for embarassment).
   Ṁgányiu! — That's okay.

10. **Máhfàahnsaai néih la!** — Thank you for your help. the
    Ṁmáh fàahn! — No problem at all.

11. **Mahnhauh néih māmìh la!** — Give my regards to your mother.
    Yáuhsàm la! — That's very kind of you.

12. **Chéng chóh!** — Please have a seat.
    Ṁgòi! — Thank you.

13. **Chéng yám chàh!** — Please have some tea.
    Ṁgòi! — Thank you.

14. **Gùnghéi faatchòih!** — Happy Chinese New Year!
    (I wish you good fortune.)

15. **Jūk néih sàn nìhn faailohk!** — I wish you a happy New Year!
    (calendar year or Chinese year)

16. **Jūk néih sàn nìhn sàantái gihhōng!**   Good health in the New Year!

    Maahnsih yùhyi!   Hoping all your wishes come true.
    Daaihgà dōu gám wah lā.   Wishing you the same.

17. **Gùnghéi faatchòih!**   Happy Chinese New Year!
    Laihsih dauhlàih!   Give me "laihsih," please!
    ("Laisih"is a money gift in a small red envelope.)

18. **Jūk néih sàangyaht faailohk!**   Wishing you a happy birthday!
    Dòjeh!   Thank you!

19. **Gùnghéi, gùnghéi!**   Congratulations!

20. **Gònbùi!**   Bottoms up!

VOCABULARY

Néih hóu ma?   How are you?

Géi hóu, yáuhsàm.   Fine.

Néih nē?   And how are you?

Màhmádéi la (gwodākheui).   So-so.

Jóusàhn!   Good morning!

Jóutáu!	Good night!
Joigin! Bāaibaai!	Good-bye. Bye-bye.
Dòjeh!	Thank you (for gift).
M̀sái haakhei!	You're welcome.
M̀gòi! M̀gòisaai!	Thank you (for service).
M̀sáim̀gòi!	Don't mention it.
Deuim̀jyuh!	Sorry!
M̀gán yiu!	That's okay.
M̀hóuyisi!	Sorry (for embarassment).
máhfàahnsaai	trouble
mahnhauh	give regards
māmìh	mother
chéng	please
chóh	have a seat
yám chàh	have some tea
Gùnghéi faatchòih!	Happy Chinese New Year ! (I wish you good fortune).

jūk	wish
sàn nìhn	new year
faailohk	happy
sàntái	body
gihhōng	health
Maahnsih yùhyi!	Hoping all your wishes come true.
Daaihgà dōu gám wah lā.	Wishing you the same.
Laihsih dauhlàih!	Give me "laihsih," please!
sàangyaht	birthday
Gùnghéi!	Congratulations!
Gònbùi!	Cheers! Bottoms up!

TRANSLATION

問候，多謝同新年祝願

Mahnhauh, Dòjeh tùhng Sàn Nìhn Jūk Yuhn

1. 你好嗎？

   幾好，有心，你呢？

   麻麻地啦！

2. 早晨！

3. 早唞！

4. 再見！

   拜拜！

5. 多謝！

   好話啦！唔使客氣！

6. 唔該！

   唔使唔該！

7. 唔該晒！

8. 對唔住！

   唔緊要！

9. 唔好意思！

   唔緊要！

10. 麻煩晒你啦！

    唔麻煩！

11. 問候你媽咪啦！

    有心！

12. 請坐！

    唔該！

13. 請飲茶！

    唔該！

14. 恭喜發財！

15. 祝你新年快樂！

16. 祝你新年身體健康！

    萬事如意！

    大家都咁話啦！

17. 恭喜發財！

    利是逗嚟！

18. 祝你生日快樂！

19. 恭喜，恭喜！

20. 乾杯！

LEVEL 2

DIALOGUES

Gaasiuh
Making Introductions

A. Ṁgòi, ngóh wán Wàhn Wáih sìnsàang.   Excuse me, I'm here to see Mr. Wong Wai.

B. Chéngmahn, néih haih bīnwái?   May I have your name, please?

A. Ngóh haih Léih Meih Lìhng. Néih haih Wòhn sìnsàang ma?   I am Mei Ling Lee. Are you Mr. Wong?

B. Haih, ngóh haih Wòhn Wáih. Kéuih haih ngóh taaitáai.   Yes. I am Wong Wai. This is my wife.

C. Néih hóu, Léih síujé.   Hello, Miss Lee.

A. Néih hóu, Wòhn táai. Nīwái haih ngóh sìnsàang Léih   Hello, Mrs. Wong. This is my husband, Gwo Hua Lee.

Gwok Wàh.

C. **M̀ hóuyisi, Léih táai, m̀haih Léih síujé.** Sorry! You are Mrs. Lee, not Miss Lee.

A. **M̀ gányiu!** That's okay.

C. **Léih sàang, Léih táai, chéng chóh la!** Mr. and Mrs. Lee, please have a seat.

A. **M̀ gòi!** Thank you.

VOCABULARY

ngóh	I
néih	you
sìnsàang	Mr.
chéngmahn	may I ask
bīnwái	who
haih	are
kéuih	he; she

taaitáai wife; Mrs.

síujé miss

m̀haih am not; is not; are not

SENTENCE PATTERNS

1. Ngóh haih Léih Meih Lìhng.
I am Mei Ling Lee.

2. Néih haih Wòhn sìnsàang ma?
Are you Mr. Wong?

3. Néih m̀haih Léih síujé. Néih haih Léih táai.
You are not Miss Lee. You are Mrs. Lee.

4. Chéng chóh la!
Please have a seat!

GRAMMAR NOTES

1. When addressing people in Cantonese, the last name comes first followed by the first name and title, i.e. , " **Wòhn Wáih sìnsàang**," *Mr. Wai Wong.* Frequently titles are shortened as in **"sàang"** for **"sìnsàang"** and **"táai"** for **"taaitáai"** i.e., **"Léih táai"** for *Mrs. Lee.*

2. Chinese verbs are not conjugated. For example, "I <u>am</u>, you <u>are</u>, he <u>is</u>, they <u>were</u>," all use the same verb **"haih."**

3. The simplest way to form a *yes/no* question is to put **"ma"** at the end of a statement.

    a) Kéuih haih Wáih sìnsàang.   *He is Mr. Wong.*

      Kéuih hai Wáih sìnsàang <u>ma</u>?   *Is he Mr. Wong?*

    b) Ngóh yiu chàh.   *I would like tea.*

      Néih yiu chàh <u>ma</u>?   *Would you like tea?*

TRANSLATION

介紹   Gaaisiuh

A. 唔該，我搵黃偉先生。

B. 請問你係邊位？

A. 我係李美玲。

你係黃先生嗎？

B. 係，我係黃偉。

佢係我太太。

你好，李小姐。

A. 你好，黃太。

呢位係我先生李國華。

C. 唔好意思，李太，

唔係李小姐。

A. 唔緊要！

C. 李生，李太，請坐！

A. 唔該！

UNIT 2

Gàtìhng tùhng Jīkyihp
Family and Occupations

A.	Néih ngūkkéi yáuh mātyéh yàhn?	Who is in your family?
B.	Yáuh bàhbā, màhmā, yāt go agō, yāt go gājē . . .	I have a father, a mother, an elder brother, an elder sister . . .
A.	Néih yáuh móuh dàihdái mùihmúi a?	Do you have younger brothers and sisters?
B.	Móuh.	No, I don't.
A.	Néih yáuh móuh jáinéui?	Do you have children?
B.	Móuh. Ngóh meihgitfān. Ngóh yáuh nàahm pàhngyáuh.	No, I'm not married. I have a boyfriend.
A.	M̀hóuyisi. Ngóh ngūkkéi yáuh taaitáai, yāt go jái	Oh, sorry. I have a wife, a son, and a daughter.

tùhng yāt go néui.

B.	Chéngmahn, néih jouh mātyéh gúngjok a?	What kind of work do you do?
A.	Ngóh haih sèungyàhn. Néih nē?	I'm a businessman. And you?
B.	Ngóh haih leuhtsī. Néih taaitáai jouh mātyéh gùngjok?	I'm a lawyer. What kind of work does your wife do?
A.	Kéuih móuh jouhyéh. Néih nàahm pàhngyáuh jouh mātyéh gùngjok a?	She doesn't work. What kind of work does your boyfriend do?
B.	Kéuih yauh haih leuhtsī.	He is also a lawyer.

VOCABULARY

ngūkkéi	family; home
yáuh	have
mātyéh	what
yáhn	person
bàhbā	father

màhmā	mother
agō	elder brother
gājē	elder sister
dàihdái	younger brother
mùihmúi	younger sister
móuh	don't
jáinéui	children
meihgitfān	not married
nàahm pàhngyáuh	boyfriend
jái	son
néui	daughter
jouh	do
gùngjok	work
sèungyàhn	businessman
leuhtsī	lawyer
móuh jouhyéh	doesn't work
yauh haih	also
tùhng	and

SENTENCE PATTERNS

1. **Ngóh ngūkkéi yáuh bàhbā, màhmā, tùhng agō.**
   I have a father, a mother, and an elder brother.

2. **Néih yáuh móuh jáinéui?**
   Do you have children?

3. **Néih jouh mātyéh gùngjok a?**
   What kind of work do you do?

4. **Ngóh haih sèungyàhn. Néih nē?**
   I'm a businessman. And you?

GRAMMAR NOTES

1. The word order of "w" questions *(who, what, when, which, where)* is reversed in Cantonese. For example, *"Who are you?"* in English comes out as ***"You are who?"*** in Cantonese. The illustration in the previous dialogue asked the question, *"What kind of work do you do?"* in Cantonese it is posed as ***"You do what kind of work?"*** **"Néih jouh mātyéh gùngjok a?"**

2. Please note that "w" questions in Cantonese end with **"a"**.

a)   **Dímyéung chìngfū a?**

How should I address you?

b)   **Néih heui bīndouh a?**

Where are you going?

3. Cantonese nouns do not use articles such as *"a, an"* or *"the"* and do not have plural forms.

4. The English sentence pattern of **Subject + Verb + Object** is identical in Cantonese. The sentence , *"I have a father"* translates directly as **"Ngóh yáuh bàhbā."** Note that when forming a question involving possession, i.e., using *"have" (yauh),* the phrase *"yauh móuh"* must be used. *"Do you have a father?"* is **"Néih yáuh móuh bàhbā?"**

TRANSLATION

家庭同職業   **Gàtìng tuhng Jīkyhp**

A. 你屋企有乜嘢人？

B. 有爸爸、媽媽、一個亞哥，一個家姊⋯⋯

A. 你有冇弟弟妹妹呀？

B. 冇。

A. 你有冇仔女？

B. 冇。我未結婚，我有男朋友。

A. 唔好意思！

我屋企有太太，一個仔同一個女。

B. 請問，你做乜嘢工作？

A. 我係商人。你呢？

B. 我係律師。你太太做乜嘢工作？

A. 佢冇做嘢。

你男朋友做乜嘢工作？

B. 佢又係律師。

Gaaisiuh Tùhngsìh

Introduction of Colleagues

A. Nīdouh haih ngóhge séjihlàuh. Nīwái haih Johnson sìnsàang. Kéuih haih méihgwok sèungyàhn. Nīwái haih Chàhn síujé, Johnson sìnsàang ge beisyù. Kéuih haih Tòihwāan yàhn.

Here is my office. This is Mr. Johnson. He is an American businessman. This is Miss Chan, Mr. Johnson's secretary. She is Taiwanese.

B. Gówái sìngsàang haih bīngo?

Who is that gentleman?

A. Kéuih haih ngóhge líhngdouh.

He is my leader.

B. Mātyéh wá?

What?

A. Ṁ hòuyisi, kéuih haih ngóhge bōsí. **Daaihluhk yàhn giu lóuhbáan jouh "líhngdouh."**

Oh, sorry. He is my boss. Mainland Chinese call a boss a "leader."

B. Géidākyi bo.

Oh, that's interesting.

A. Chéngmahn, néih gwai sing?

Excuse me, what's your last name?

B. Ngóh sing Hòh.

My last name is Ho.

A. Dímyéung chìngfū a?

How should I address you?

B. Giu gnóh jouh Síu Hòh la.

Call me Siu Ho.

A. Chéng chóh la, Síu Hòh.

Please have a seat, Siu Ho.

VOCABULARY

nīdouh	here
ngóhge	my
séjihlàuh	office
méihgwok yàhn	American
beisyù	secretary

Tòihwāan yàhn	Taiwanese
bīngo	who
gówái	that
líhngdou	leader
Mātyéh wá?	What?
bōsí; lóuhbáan	boss
Daaihluhk yàhn	Mainland Chinese
Géidākyi bo.	Oh, that's interesting.
gwai sing	last name
dímyéung	how
chìngfū	address (you)
giu gnóh jouh	call me . . .

SENTENCE PATTERNS

1. **Nīdouh haih ngóhge séjihlàuh.**
   Here is my office.

2. **Kéuih haih chàhn síujé, Johnson sìnsàang ge beisyù.**
   She is Miss Chan, Mr. Johnson's secretary.

3. **Chéngmahn, néih gwai sing?**
   Excuse me, what's your last name?

4. **Dímyéung chìngfū a?**
   How should I address you?

GRAMMAR NOTES

1. Possessives (*my, your, mine, his, her*) are formed in Cantonese by adding "**ge**" to nouns and pronouns, i.e., **ngóh** (I) - ngóhge (my), néih (you) - **néihge (your)**, **kéuih** (he, she) - **kéuihge (his, her)**, etc.

2. The only exception to this is when referring to members of your own family, rather than saying *"my" (ngóhge) wife*, you say *"I" (ngóh) wife*.

3. Nationalities are formed by combining the name of the country with the noun for *"man"* as in ***Jùnggwok yàhn***, *China man* or ***Méihgwok yàhn,*** *America man.*

4. To indicate mild commands, requests or suggestions add **"la"** to the last words of the sentence. For example:

> **Chéng chóh la!**
>
> *Have a seat!*
>
> **Béi būi chàh ngóh la!**
>
> *Would you give me a cup of tea, please!*
>
> **Chéng chēutheui la!**
>
> *Please get out!*

TRANSLATION

介紹同事　Gaaisiuh Tùhngsìh

A. 呢喥係我嘅寫字樓。

呢位係莊晨生。

佢係美國商人。

呢位係陳小姐，莊晨生嘅秘書，佢係台灣人。

B. 嗰位先生係邊個？

A. 佢係我嘅領導。

B. 乜嘢話？

A. 唔好意思，佢係我波士，大陸人叫老闆做 " 領導 "。

B. 幾得意嘞！

A. 請問，你貴姓？

B. 我姓何。

A. 點樣稱呼呀？

B. 叫我做小何啦！

A. 請坐啦，小何！

UNIT 4

Hái Gafē Chāansāt
Ordering at a Coffee Shop

A. **Sìnsàang, yám dī mātyéh?** Sir, what would you like to drink?

B. **Yáuh nìhngmùng chàh ma?** Do you have lemon tea?

A. **Yáuh, yiu géi būi?** Yes. How many cups do you want?

B. **Yāt būi géi chín?** How much is a cup?

A. **Chāt hòuh bun jí .** Seventy-five cents.

B. **Hóu, yiu yāt būi. Yaúh móuh hólohk?** Okay. One, please. Do you have Coke?

A. **Deuimjyuh, maaihsaai la. Chàthéi hóu ma?** Sorry, sold out. How about 7-Up?

B. **Hóu lā, yāt būi chàthéi gā bīng. Yáuh móuh daahngòu a?** Okay. A glass of 7-Up with ice. Do you have cake?

A. Yáuh, yiu géi gauh?	Yes, we do. How many pieces do you want?
B. Léuhng gauh.	Two.
A. Juhng yiu dī mātyéh?	Anything else?
B. Móuh la, yātguhng gèi chín?	No. How much all together?
A. Sàam go baat hòuh luhk.	$3.86.
B. Nàh, nīdouh haih sahp mān.	Here is a ten dollar bill.
A. Jáaufàan luhk go yāt hòuh sei. Dòjeh saai néih.	Here is $6.14. Thank you very much.
B. Bāaibaai.	Bye-bye.

VOCABULARY

nìhngmùng	lemon
géi būi	how many cups
yiu	want, would like
maaihsaai	sold out
daahngòu	cake

gauh	piece
léuhng gauh	two pieces
Juhng yiu dī mātyéh?	Anything else?
nīdouh haih	here is
jáaufàan	give change
Jáaufàan luhk go yāt hòuh sei.	Here is $6.14.

SUPPLEMENTARY WORDS

yámbán	drinks
jàaifè	black coffee
hèungbàn (jáu)	champagne
gàiméihjáu	cocktail
sàangbè	draught beer
sìnnáaih	fresh milk
gwójàp	fruit juice

jaahpgwó bànjih	fruit punch
kwongchyùhnséui	mineral water
cháangjāp	orange juice
wàisihgeih	whisky
bējáu	beer
Chìngdóu bējáu	Tsing Tao beer
fòngtòhng	sugar cubes
syùhtíu	French fries
fótéui	ham
honbóubàau	hamburger
yihtgáu	hot dog
gwójeung	jam
yidaaihleih bohkbéng	pizza
boudīng	pudding
sàléut	salad
sàammàhnjih	sandwich

SENTENCE PATTERNS

1. **Yáuh nìhngmùng chàh ma?**
   Do you have lemon tea?

2. **Yáuh, yiu géi būi?**
   How many cups do you want?

3. **Yāt būi géi chín?**
   How much is a cup?

4. **Ngóh yiu yāt būi Chàthéi gā bīng.**
   I'd like a glass of 7-Up with ice.

5. **Juhng yiu dī mātyéh?**
   Anything else?

6. **Móuh la, yātguhng gèi chín?**
   No. How much all together?

GRAMMAR NOTES

Measure Words

1. We noted earlier that Cantonese does not use articles such as *"a, an, the."* It is necessary, however, to use another system to indicate a thing such as a or one child, a book, a car, etc. Cantonese uses words with nouns to make those distinctions. These are called measure words. There are about 20 most frequently used measure words and they are used to identify groups of words by certain characteristics.

2. For example, the measure word *"go"* is used with nouns denoting persons and things which are round in appearance.

yāt go yàhn	(a person)
yāt go mihnbāau	(a bread)
yāt go jūng	(a clock)

3. Following are some common measure words for food and drink:

búi	*(cup, glass of)*	(tea, coffee, wine, water, beer)
gun	*(can of)*	(Coca Cola, 7-Up, beer)
go		(apple, orange, peach, steamed bun, hot dog)
jek		(banana, book, plate, spoon)
wún		(rice, soup, porridge, noodle)
dihp		(fried rice, fried noodle)

喺咖啡餐室　　Hái Gafē Chāansāt

A. 先生，飲啲乜嘢？

B. 有檸檬茶嗎？

A. 有，要幾杯？

B. 一杯幾錢？

A. 七毫半紙。

B. 好，要一杯。

　　有冇可樂？

A. 對唔住，賣晒啦！

　　七喜好嗎？

B. 好啦，一杯七喜加冰。

　　有冇蛋糕呀？

A. 有，要幾嚿？

B. 兩嚿 。

A. 重要啲乜嘢？

B. 冇了，一共幾錢？

A. 三個八毫六。

B. 那，呢道係十蚊。

A. 找番六個一毫四。

多謝晒你！

B. 拜拜！

UNIT 5

Sāanggwó tùhng Gachìhn
Fruit and Prices

A. M̀ gòi, pòuhtàihjí géi chín yāt bohng?

How much for a pound of grapes?

B. Yih sahp sei māan.

HK$24.00.

A. Béi yāt bohng làih lā.

May I have a pound, please?

B. Pìhnggwó hóu leng a. Sahp māan yāt bohng.

The apples are nice. HK$10.00 a pound.

A. M̀ yiu, ngóh ngūkkéi juhng yáuh pìhnggwó. Cháang tìhm m̀tìhm a?

No, I don't want any. I have apples at home. Are the oranges sweet?

B. Hóu tìhm ga! Haih méihgwok ge Sànkèihsih cháang. Yih sahp yih māan yāt dā.

Very sweet. These are Sunkist oranges from America. HK$22.00 a dozen.

A. **Béi bun dā làih lā.**　　　Give me a half dozen.

B. **Juhng yiu dī mātyéh**　　Would you like any other fruit?
   sāanggwó? Mònggwó tùhng　Mangoes and watermelons are all
   sàigwà dōu hóu leng a.　very nice.

A. **Mònggwó géi chín yāt go?**　How much for a mango?

B. **Luhk mān yāt go, luhk sap**　HK$6.00 a piece. HK$60.00 a
   mān yāt dā.　　　　dozen.

A. **Yiu bun dā gau la.**　　Half a dozen is enough.

B. **Juhng yiu dī mātyéh?**　　Anything else?

A. **M̀ yiu la, gau la. Yātguhng**　I don't want any more. That's
   géi chín?　　　　enough. How much is it all
   　　　　　　　　together?

B. **Hahmbaahnglaahng haih**　The total is HK$65.00.
   luhk sahp ńgh mān.

A. **Nīdouh haih yāt baak mān.**　Here is a HK$100 bill.

B. **Nàh, jáaufàan sàam sahp**　Here is HK$35.00 change. Thank
   ńgh mān. Dòjehsaai néih.　you very much.

A. **M̀ gòisaai! Báaibaai!**　　Thank you. Bye-bye.

VOCABULARY

pòuhtàihjí	grape
géi chín	how much
bohng	pound
béi	give, May I have . . .
pìhnggwó	apple
leng	nice, beautiful
m̀yiu	don't want
cháang	orange
tìhm	sweet
hóu	good, (very)
Sànkèihsih cháang	Sunkist orange
yāt dā	a dozen
bun	half
juhng	still, yet

sāanggwó	fruit
mònggwó	mango
sàigwà	watermelon
dōu	all
gau	enough
yātguhng; hahmbaahnglaahng	all together
júngsou	total
yāt baak	one hundred
mān; ngàhnchín	dollar
jáaufàan	give change

SENTENCE PATTERNS

1. **Pòuhtàihjí géi chín yāt bohng?**
    How much for a pound of grapes?

2. **Béi yāt bohng làih lā.**
    May I have a pound, please?

3. **Pìhnggwó hóu leng a.**
    The apples are nice.

4. **Yiu bun dā gau la.**
    Half a dozen is enough.

5. **Nīdouh haih yāt baak mān.**
    Here is a HK$100 bill.

6. **Jáaufàan sàam sahp ńgh mān.**
    Here is HK$35.00 change.

GRAMMAR NOTES

1. Adjectives, prices, dates or weekdays placed after a subject eliminate the need for the verb form **"to be"** *(haih.)*

   a) **Pìhnggwó hóu leng.**

   The apples are nice.

   b) **Yāt dā cháang yih sahp yih mān.**

   A dozen of oranges are 22 dollars.

   c) **Gàmyaht Láihbaaingh.**

   Today is Friday.

2. How to read prices in Cantonese

   a) 1-9 cents *sīn*

0.01	**yāt go sīn**	**yat fān (chìhn)**
0.02	**léuhng go sīn**	**léuhng fān (chìhn)**
.....		
0.09	**gáu go sīn**	**gau fān (chìhn)**

   In Hong Kong *"sīn"* is used for cents; in Canton *"fān"* or *"fān chìhn"* is used.

   b) 10-90 cents in units of ten   **hòuh** *or* **hòuhjí**

0.10	**yāt hòuh**
0.20	**léung hòuh**
...	
0.90	**gáu hòuh**

c) 11-19 cents

  0.11 **hòuh yāt**

  0.12 **hòuh yih**

  .....

  0.19 **hòuh gáu**

d) Cents from 21-99

  0.22 **léuhng hòuh yih**

  0.33 **sàam hòuh sàam**

  0.44 **sei hòuh sei**

  0.58 **ńgh hòuh baat**

e) How 5 is expressed colloquially

  0.15 **(yāt) hòuh bun**

  0.25 **léuhng hòuh bun**

  0.35 **sàam hòuh bun**

  0.55 **ńgh hòuh bun**

Note: "bun" means "half" and is used colloquially to express five.

f) Dollars *Mān or ngàhnchín*

  1.00 **yāt mān**

  2.00 **léuhng mān**

  22.00 **yih sahp yih mān**

  35.00 **sàam sahp ńgh mān**

"Mān" is used to express dollars. *"Ngàhnchín"* is also used for *"dollars"*, but is an older expression.

g) Compound Money

Dollars *go* **tens of cents** *hòuh* **cents**

3.22	sàam *go* leuhng *hòuh* yih
1.63	yāt *go* luhk *hòuh* sàam
2.45	léuhng *go* sei *hòuh* bun
42.15	sei sahp yih *go* yāt *hòuh* bun
99.05	gáu sahp gáu *go* lìhng ńgh

Note: 0.05 is expressed as zero five (lihng ńgh)

TRANSLATION

生果同價錢　　Sāanggwó tùhng Gachìhn

A. 唔該，葡提子幾錢一磅？

B. 二十四蚊。

A. 比一磅嚟啦！

B. 蘋果好靚呀，十蚊一磅。

A. 唔要，我屋企重有蘋果。橙甜唔甜呀？

B. 好甜㗎！係美國嘅新奇士橙。二十二蚊一打。

A. 比半打嚟啦！

B. 重要啲乜嘢生果？芒果同西瓜都好靚呀！

A. 芒果幾錢一個？

B. 六蚊一個，六十蚊一打。

A. 要半打夠啦。

B. 重要啲乜嘢？

A. 唔要啦，夠啦！一共幾錢？

B. 一共六十五蚊。

A. 呢道係一百蚊。

B. 那，找番三十五蚊。多謝晒你！

A. 唔該晒！拜拜！

Sihkbán tùhng Yámbán
Food and Drink

**A. Ngóh jùngyi yám gafē,
mhaih hóu jùngyi yám chàh.**

I like to drink coffee. I don't like to drink tea too much.

**B. Ngóhdeih jùnggwokyàhn
jùngyi yám chàh.**

We Chinese like to drink tea.

A. Néih jùng mjùngyi yám jáu?

Do you like to drink wine?

**B. Ngóh jùngyi yám bējáu tùhng
hùhngjáu.**

I like to drink beer and red wine.

**A. Ngóh jùngyi yám
Hóháuhólohk tùhng Chàthéi.**

I like Coca-Cola and 7-Up.

**B. Néihdeih sāiyàhn jóuchāan
sihk mātyéh?**

What do you westerners eat for breakfast?

**A. Dòsí gā ngàuhyàuh waahkjé
gwójeung, cháangjāp, cháh**

Toast with butter or jam, orange juice, tea or coffee. How about you

waahkjé gafē. Néihdeih tòhngyàhn nē?	Chinese?
B. Ngóhdeih sihk mihn waahkjé mihnbāau. Yáuhsìh heui chàhlàuh yám cháh.	We eat noodles or bread. Sometimes we go to the teahouse to drink tea.
A. M̀ haih gwa, heui chàhlàuh jihng haih yám chàh?	No kidding! You go to the teahouse just to drink tea?
B. Ngóhdeih Gwóngdùngyàhn góng heui yám chàh jīkhaih heui sihk dím-sàm a!	When we Cantonese say we're going to the teahouse, we mean we're going there to eat dim sum.
A. Ngóh jàn haih "mùhng chàh chàh!"	I didn't know about that.

VOCABULARY

jùngyi	like
yám	drink
gafē	coffee
m̀h haih hóu jùngyi	don't like it too much
chàh	tea

ngóhdeih	we
jùnggwokyàhn; tòhngyàhn	Chinese
jáu	wine
bējáu	beer
hùhngjáu	red wine
Hóháuhólohk	Coca-Cola
Chàthéi	7-Up
sāiyàhn	westerner
sihk	eat
jóuchāan	breakfast
dòsí	toast
gā	with
ngàuhyàuh	butter
gwójeung	jam
cháangjāp	orange juice
mihn	noodle

mihnbāau	bread
yáuhsìh	sometimes
heui	go
chàhlàuh	tea house
M̀ haih gwa!	No kidding!
waahkjé	or (in a statement)
dihnghaih	or (in a question)
góng	say, speak
jīkhaih	mean
dím-sàm	dim sum
Ngóh jàn haih "mùhng chàh chàh!"	I didn't know about that.

SENTENCE PATTERNS

1. **Ngóhdeih jùnggwokyàhn jùngyi yám chàh.**
   We Chinese like to drink tea.

2. **Ngóh m̀haih hóu jùngyi yám chàh.**
   I don't like to drink tea too much.

3. **Néih jùng m̀jùngyi yám jáu?**
   Do you like to drink wine?

4. **Jùngyi.**
   Yes, I do.

5. **Néihdeih sāiyàhn jóuchāan sihk mātyéh?**
   What do you westerners eat for breakfast?

GRAMMAR NOTES

One of the charming aspects of Cantonese is in the way certain questions are formed. In English we would, for example, ask *"Are you Joe?"* In Cantonese the form is affirmative negative, **"You are/are not Joe?"** The letter **"m̀"** is used with the verb to denote negative as in **haih** *(are)* **m̀haih** *(are not.)*

Another example is *"Are you going?"* In Cantonese this becomes *"You are going/not going?"* **Neih heui m̀heui?**

An exception is the word **"yáuh"** *(to have).* Its negative is **"móuh"** and together they form a question **(yáuh móuh...?)**

Two syllable verbs or verb-noun phrases are split when put into the affirmative/negative question form.

> **"jùngyi"** *(like)* is put into question form as **"jùng m̀jùngyi?"**

> **"sihk dímsùm"** *(eat dimsum)* - **"sihk m̀sihk dímsùm?"**

You will have to learn these variations as you meet them without cluttering your mind with rules.

TRANSLATION

食品同飲品   Sihkbán tùhng Yámbán

A. 我鍾意飲咖啡，唔係好鍾意飲茶。

B. 我哋中國人鍾意飲茶。

A. 你鍾唔鍾意飲酒？

B. 我鍾意飲啤酒同紅酒。

A. 我鍾意飲可口可樂同七喜。

B. 你哋西人早餐食乜嘢？

A. 多士加牛油或者果醬，橙汁，茶或者咖啡。

你地唐人呢？

B. 我哋食麵或者麵包。有時去茶樓飲茶。

A. 唔係呱，去茶樓淨係飲茶？

B. 我哋廣東人講去飲茶即係去食點心呀！

A. 我真係蒙查查！

UNIT 7

Dihnwá Houhmáh
Telephone Number

A. Ǹgòi, néih baahngūngsāt ge dihnwá haih géi houh a?

Excuse me, what's your office telephone number?

B. Sàam baat yāt - baat yih ńgh yih.

381-8252.

A. Mātyéh wá? Ǹgòi, chéng góng maahn dīt lā.

What? Excuse me, please speak slowly.

B. Sáam baat yāt - baat yih ńgh yih.

381-8252.

A. Dāk la, máhfàahnsaai néih la.

Okay. Sorry for the trouble.

B. Néih ngūkkéi ge dihnwá haih géi houh?

What's your home phone number?

A. Deuiṁjyuh, ngóh ngūkkéi **móuh dihnwá, chéng dálàih** **ngóh gùngsì - baat ńgh luhk-** **gáu gáu yih gáu.**

Sorry, I don't have a home phone. Please call me at work. My company's phone number is 856-9929.

B. Chéngmahn, néih haih ṁhaih **ngoihgwokyàhn a?**

Excuse me, are you a foreigner?

A. Haih,ngóh haih fàangwáilóu. **Ngóh haih Yìnggwok yàhn.**

Yes, I am "faangwailou." I am British.

B. Néihge Gwóngdùngwá góng **dāk géi hóu bo.**

You speak Cantonese very well.

A. Gwojéung, gwojéung. Ngóh **jí sīk góng síu síu.**

Thank you for the compliment. I can only speak a little.

VOCABULARY

dihnwá	telephone
houh	number
góng	speak
maahn	slowly
dálàih	call

gùngsì	company
ngoihgwok yàhn; **fàangwáilóu; lóuhfaàn**	foreigner
Yìnggwok yàhn	British
Gwóngdùngwá	Cantonese
gwojéung	to compliment; to flatter
sīk	can
jí	only
síu síu	little

SENTENCE PATTERNS

1. **M̀goi, néih baahngūngsāt ge dihnwá haih géi houh a?**
   Excuse me, what's your office telephone number?

2. **M̀goi, chéng góng maahn dīt lā.**
   Excuse me, please speak slowly.

3. **Néihge Gwóngdùngwá góng dāk géi hóu bo.**
   You speak Cantonese very well.

4. **Ngóh jí sīk góng síu síu.**
   I can only speak a little.

GRAMMAR NOTES

"Dāk" is a very useful word which roughly translates as requesting permission.

    "Dāk La!" used in the dialogue means *"OK!"*

    "Dāk m̀dāk a?" means *"Is this alright?"*

It is also used as an add-on after a verb.

    "Ngóh dāk m̀dāk jáu a?"

    May I leave now?

87

"Ngóh jáu dāk meih a?"

May I leave now?

"Dāk meih" is used here in the same sense as **"dāk m̀dāk."**

TRANSLATION

電話號碼 Dihnwá Houhmáh

A. 唔該，你辦公室嘅電話係幾號呀？

B. 381-8252。

A. 乜嘢話？唔該，講慢啲啦！

B. 381-8252。

A. 得啦！麻煩晒你啦！

B. 你屋企嘅電話係幾號？

A. 對唔住。我屋企冇電話，請打嚟我公司 — 856-9929。

B. 請問，你係唔係外國人呀？

A. 係，我係番鬼佬。我係英國人。

B. 你嘅廣東話講得幾好�！

A. 過獎，過獎！我只識講少少！

Sìngkèih tùhng Yeukgin

Weekdays and Making an Appointment

A. Wái, gàmyaht haih láihbaai géi a?

Hello, what day is today?

B. Láihbaaiyih.

Tuesday.

A. Néih tìngyaht dāk m̀dākhàahn a?

Are you available tomorrow?

B. Deuim̀jyuh, m̀dākhàahn. Yáuh mātyeh sih a?

Sorry, I'm not available. What's going on?

A. Ngóh séung tùhng néih kìng sàangyi. Láihbaaisei dāk m̀dākhàahn?

I want to discuss business with you. Are you available on Thursday?

B. Láihbaaisei yauh haih hóu mòhng. Seuhngjau yiu gin

I am also busy on Thursday. I'm meeting clients in the morning and yàhnhaak, hahjau yiu hòiwúi. | in the afternoon I have a meeting.

A. Néih jàn haih go daaih
mòhng yàhn. Sìngkèinhńgh
jùngnǵh dākhàahn ma? | Oh, you are really busy! How about Friday at noon?

B. Chùhng sahpyāt dím dou yāt
dím ngóh dākhàahn. | I'm available from 11:00 a.m. to 1:00 p.m.

A. Yātchàih heui sihk ngaanjau
lā. Ngóh chéng néih. | Then let's go for lunch. It's my treat.

B. M̀sái gáhm haakhei la. | You don't have to do that.

A. Bīnsihk bīnkìng ma. Ngóh
sahpyāt dím làih wán néih
yātchàih heui la. | We could talk while we're having lunch. I'll be there at 11:00 and we can go together.

B. Hóu la. | Okay.

VOCABULARY

wái	hello (on telephone)
gàmyaht	today
láihbaai géi	what day

láihbaaiyih	Tuesday
tìngyaht	tomorrow
dākhàahn	available
Yáuh mātyeh sih a?	What's going on?
séung	want
tùhng	with
kìng	discuss
sàangyi	business
láihbaaisei	Thursday
hóu mòhng	very busy
gin yàhnhaak	meet clients
yiu hòiwúi	have a meeting
jàn haih	really
jùngnǵh	noon
sìngkèinhnǵh; láihbaainǵh	Friday
chùhng	from

dou	to
yātchàih; yātchái	let's
ngaanjau	lunch
Ngóh chéng néih.	It's my treat.
Ṁsái gáhm haakhei la.	You don't have to do that.
bīn	while

SENTENCE PATTERNS

1. **Néih tìngyaht dāk m̀dākhàahn a?**
   Are you available tomorrow?

2. **Chùhng sahpyāt dím dou yāt dím ngóh dākhàahn.**
   I'm available from 11:00 a.m. to 1:00 p.m.

3. **Yātchàih heui sihk ngaanjau lā.**
   Let's go for lunch.

4. **Ngóh sahpyāt dím làih wán néih yātchàih heui la.**
   I'll be there at 11:00 and we can go together.

5. **Ngóh chéng néih.**
   It's my treat.

GRAMMAR NOTES

1. **Weekdays**

In the Western world, Sunday is counted as the first day of the week, but in the Chinese world Monday is the first weekday. The days of the week are simply numbered. The Cantonese word "Láibaai" means "week" and "Sunday. " To name the weekday beginning with Monday as day one, just add the number to "Láihbaai. "

Monday	**Láihbaaiyāt**
Tuesday	**Láihbaaiyih**
Wednesday	**Láihbaaisàam**
Thursday	**Láihbaaisei**
Friday	**Láihbaaingh**
Saturday	**Láihbaailuhk**

2. Months

Months are as simple as weekdays. The word *"yuht"* means month. Just put the number of the month with *"yuht"* and you have it.

Yātyuht	January
Yihyuht	February
Sàamyuht	March
Seiyuht	April
Nghyuht	May
Luhkyuht	June
Chātyuht	July
Baatyuht	August
Gáuyuht	September
Sahpyuht	October
Sahpyātyuht	November
Sahpyihyuht	December

To specify the number of months, the word *"yuht"* is modified by the measure word for numbers *"go."* So, *"baat go yuht"* means eight months; *"sei go yuht"* is four months.

3. Years

In Cantonese the number of the year is read out as four separate numbers plus the word *"nìhn"* for year.

> 1989   **yāt gáu baat gáu nìhn**

The date, month and year in Cantonese are given in a different order than in American English.

British English	5-8-1994	**Eighth of May, 1994**
American English	8-5-1994	**May 8th, 1994**
Cantonese	1994-8-5	**yāt gáu gáu sei nìhn**
		baatyuht ng̀h houh

TRANSLATION

星期同約見   Sìngkèih tùhng Yeukgin

A. 喂，今日係禮拜幾？

B. 禮拜二。

A. 你嚟日得唔得閑？

B. 對唔住，唔得閑。有乜嘢事呀？

A. 我想同你傾生意。禮拜四得唔得閑？

B. 禮拜四又係好忙。上晝要見客，下晝要開會。

A. 你真係個大忙人。星期五中午得閑嗎？

B. 從十一點到一點我得閑。

A. 一齊去食晏晝啦！我請你。

B. 唔使咁客氣啦！

A. 邊食邊傾啦！我十一點嚟搵你一齊去啦！

B. 好啦！

Jùng choi
Chinese Food

A. Néih jùng m̀jùngyi sihk
   Gwóngdùng choi a?

Do you like Cantonese cuisine?

B. Jùngyi. Ngóh jeui júngyi
   Gùngbóugāidìng, sàilàahnfà
   cháau ngàuhyuhk tùhng
   syùnlaaht tòng.

Yes, I do. I like Kung Pao chicken, beef with broccoli, and hot and sour soup most.

A. Gódī dōu m̀haih Gwóngdùng
   choi, haih Bākgìng choi.

Those are not Cantonese dishes. They are Beijing cuisine.

B. Ngóh yauh jùngyi wòtip,
   chēungyún tùhng cháau
   mihn.

I like potstickers, spring rolls and chow mein.

A. Gódī dōu haih bākfōng
   síusihk.

Oh, those are all Northern Chinese foods.

B. Gám, bīndī haih Gwóngdùng
   choi a?

Then, what is Cantonese cuisine?

97

A. **Baahkjáaumgài, chìngjìng sehkbāan yú, baahkcheuhà. Dáng ngóh hahchi chéng néih sihk "Gáu Daaih Gwái."**

Boiled chicken, steamed garoupa (grouper), poached shrimp. Next time let me take you for "Gáu Daaih Gwái."

B. **Mātyéh wá? "Gáu Daaih Gwái?" Neihdeih Gwóngdùngyàhn sihk "Gwái?"**

What? "Nine big ghosts?" You Cantonese eat ghosts?

A. **"Gáu Daaih Gwái" haih yáuh gáu dihp sung ge jáujihk a.**

"Gáu Daaih Gwái" is a banquet with nine courses.

B. **Ngóh jàn haih "Mùhng chàh chàh." Hóu lā, dòjeh néih sìn.**

I didn't know about that. O.K., thank you in advance.

VOCABULARY

Gwóngdùng choi	Cantonese cuisine
Gùngbóugāidìng	Kung Pao chicken
sàilàahnfà	broccoli
ngàuhyuhk	beef
cháau	fried

syùnlaaht	sour and hot
tòng	soup
choi	dish
Bākgìng choi	Beijing cuisine
wòtip	potsticker
chēungyún	spring roll
cháau mihn	chow mein
bākfōng	Northern
síusihk	snacks
baahkjáaumgài	boiled chicken
(chìng) jìng	steam
sehkbāan	garoupa
baahkcheuhà	poached shrimp
hahchi	next time
sung	course
jáujihk	banquet
yú	fish

SUPPLEMENTARY WORDS

Gàiyùhng sùkméihgàng   Chicken and sweet corn soup

Hóisìn tòng   Seafood soup

Wàhntàn   Won-Ton soup

Yìugwó gàidìng   Diced chicken with cashew nuts

Mahttòuh hàkàuh   Stir-fried prawns with honied walnuts

Gāhèung dauhfuh   Family style Tofu

Muhksèui yuhk   Mushu pork

Bākgìng pinpèihgáap   sliced Peking duck

Nìhngmùng gài   Lemon chicken filet

SENTENCE PATTERNS

1. **Ngóh jeui júngyi Gùngbóugāidìng.**
   I like Kung Pao chicken most.

2. **Bīndi haih Gwóngdùng choi a?**
   What is Cantonese cuisine?

3. **Dáng ngóh hahchi chéng néih sihk "Gáu Daaih Gwái."**
   Next time let me take you for "Gáu Daaih Gwái."

GRAMMAR NOTES

1. *"Jeui"* indicates the superlative degree, i.e. *"the most."* Note that *"jeui"* precedes the verb and adjective.

   a. *jeui jùngyi* - literally *"most like "*

      Ngóh jeui jùngyi dímsàm.

      I like dimsum most.

   b. *Jeui leng* - *the most beautiful*

      Léih síujé jeui leng.

      Miss Lee is the most beautiful.

2. **"Chéng"** has two meanings:

a)   *"please"*

Chéng yahplàih la!

Come in, please!

Chéng tèng dihnwá!

Answer the phone, please!

b)   *"invite"* - somebody to do something

Ngóh chéng néih yám gafē.

I invite you for a cup of coffee.

Ngóh chéng néih sihk faahn.

I invite you for dinner.

2. Seven measure words you need to know for a Chinese meal and a sentence pattern for ordering a dish or requesting a plate, a bowl, a fork, etc.

M̀goi, béi   jek   wún ngóh.
            measure word

Excuse me, give me a bowl, please!

a) **jek**   **wún** *(bowl)*, **díhp** *(plate)*, **chìhgāng** *(spoon)*

b) **wún** *(bowl)*   **faahn** *(rice)*, **tòng** *(soup)*, **jùk** *(congee)*, **tòngmihn** *(noodles in soup)*

c) **dìhp** *(plate)* **sung** *(dish)*, **cháau faahn** *(fried rice)*, **cháau mihn** *(fried noodles)*

d) **deui** *(pair)*   **faaijí** *(chopsticks)*

e) **bá**   **chā** *(fork)*, **dōu** *(knife)*

f) **jēun** *(bottle)* **sihyàuh** *(soysauce)*, **wùhjìufán** *(pepper)*, **chou** *(vinegar)*

g) **bùi** *(glass)* **bīngséui** *(ice water)*, **bējáu** *(beer)*, **sàangbè** *(draught)*

TRANSLATION

中菜　　　Jùng choi

A.　你中唔鍾意食廣東菜呀？

B.　鍾意。

　　我最鍾意宮保雞丁、西蘭花炒牛肉，酸辣湯。

A.　嗰的都唔係廣東菜，係北京菜。

B.　我又鍾意鍋貼、春卷同炒麵。

A.　嗰啲係北方小食。

B.　咁，邊啲係廣東菜呀？

A.　白斬雞、清蒸石班魚、白灼蝦……等我下次請你食"九大鬼"。

B.　乜嘢話？"九大鬼"？你地廣東人食"鬼"？

A.　"九大鬼"係有九大碟餸嘅酒席呀！

B.　我真係"蒙查查"。

　　好啦，多謝你先！

Daap Fèigèi
Catching a Flight

A. Chéngmahn, yìhgā géidím?	Excuse me, what time is it now?
B. Baat dím gáu go jih.	A quarter to nine.
A. Nīdouh ge ngàhnhòhng géidímjūng hòi mùhn?	When do the banks open here?
B. Hèunggóng ge ngàhnhòhng jìujóu gáu dím hòi mùhn, hahjau ńgh dím sāan mùhn.	The banks in Hong Kong open at 9:00 a.m. and close at 5:00 p.m.
A. Ngóh yiu heui ló dī chín, m̀ji gau m̀gau jūng nē?	I need to get some money and I don't know if I have enough time.
B. Néih daap géidímjūng ge fèigèi?	When is your flight scheduled?
A. Daap sahp dím bun heui	10:30 a.m. flight 1340 to Paris.

Bàlàih ge yāt sàam sei lìhng
hòhngbāan.

B. M̀hsáigāp. Chùhng nīdouh   No need to hurry. It takes only half
daap dīksí heui gèichèuhng   an hour to get to the airport by taxi.
jíyiu bungo jūngtàuh.

A. Gám, ngóh jauh heui   In that case, I will go to the bank to
ngàhnhòhng ló chín sīn.   get some money first.

B. Jūk néih seuhnfùng!   Have a good flight!

A. Hóu wah la.   Thank you.

VOCABULARY

yìhgā	now
géidím; géidímjūng	what time
baat dím gáu go jih	a quarter to nine
ngàhnhòhng	bank
hòi mùhn	open
Hèunggóng	Hong Kong

jìujóu; seuhjau	a.m.
hahjau	p.m.
sāan mùhn	close
ló	get
dī	some
chín	money
m̀jì	don't know
daap	take
fèigèi	airplane
hòhngbāan	flight
heui	go
Bàlàih	Paris
M̀hsáigāp.	No need to hurry.
gèichèuhng	airport
dīksí	taxi
gám	in that case

sīn   first

Jūk néih seuhnfùng!   Have a good flight!

Hóu wa la.   Thank you for saying that.

SENTENCE PATTERNS

1. **Chéngmahn, yìhgā géidím?**
   Excuse me, what time is it now?

2. **Nīdouh ge ngàhnhòhng géidímjūng hòi mùhn?**
   When do the banks here open?

3. **Hèunggóng ge ngàhnhòhng jìujóu gáu dím hòi mùhn.**
   The banks in Hong Kong open at 9:00 a.m.

4. **Néih daap géidímjūng ge fèigèi?**
   When is your flight scheduled?

5. **Chùhng nīdouh daap dīksí heui gèichèuhng jíyiu bungo jūngtàuh.**
   It takes only half an hour to get to the airport by taxi.

6. **Ngóh heui ngàhnhòhng ló chín sīn.**
   I will go to the bank to get some money first.

GRAMMAR NOTES

When denoting time in Cantonese, the position of the time phrase is different from English. Where we say, for example, *"The bank opens at 9 AM.,"* in Cantonese it is **Subject + Time Phrase + Verb.** *" The bank at 9 AM opens."*

Ngàhnhòhng <u>gáu dím</u> hòi mùhn.
(time phrase)

TRANSLATION

搭飛機　　Daap Fèigèi

A. 請問，而加幾點？

B. 八點九個字。

　　（八點四十五分）

A. 呢道嘅銀行幾點鍾開門？

B. 香港嘅銀行朝早九點開門，下畫五點閂門。

A. 我要去攞錢，唔知夠唔夠鍾呢？

B. 你搭幾點鍾嘅飛機？

A. 搭十點半，去巴黎嘅1340航班。

B. 唔使急。

從呢道搭的士去機場只要半個鐘頭。

A. 咁，我就去銀行攞錢先。

B. 祝你順風！

A. 好話啦！

UNIT 11

Heui Sàangyaht Pātìh

Going to a Birthday Party

A. **Wai, heui bīnsyu a? Nìngjyuh yāt daaih bāau láihmaht.**

Hey! Where are you going with all those gifts?

B. **Heui hòi sàangyaht pātìh.**

I'm going to a birthday party.

A. **Bīngo sàangyaht a?**

Whose birthday is it?

B. **Ngóhge méihgwok pàhngyáuh Bóulòh. Gauhnín ngóhdeih yātchàih jouhsih.**

My American friend, Paul. We worked together last year.

A. **Kéuih jyuh bīndouh a? Dáng ngóh chè néih heui lā.**

Where does he live? Let me give you a ride.

B. **M̀sái la. Kéuih jyuh Gáulùhng Sàn Saigaai jáudim. Ngóh daap dīksí heui dāk la.**

That's not necessary. He's staying at the New World Hotel in Kowloon. I'll take a cab.

A. Gam haakhei. Néih géisí sàangyaht a? Dousìh ngóh sung gih láihmaht béi néih lā.

Why don't you let me drive you? When is your birthday? I'd like to give you a gift.

B. Ngóh gáu yuht sahp ńgh sàangyaht. Bātgwo m̀sái gam haakhei la. Dousìh ngóh wúih chéng néih làih ngóhge sàangyaht pātìh.

My birthday is September 15th, but there is no need to do that. I will invite you to my birthday party, though.

A. Dòjeh néih sìn. Báaibaai!

Okay, thank you in advance. Bye-bye!

VOCABULARY

Wai!	Hey!
heui	go
bīnsyu; bīndouh	where
láihmaht	gift
sàangyaht	birthday
pātìh	party
bīngoge	whose

113

jouhsih	work
gauhnín	last year
jyuh	live; stay at
dáng	let
chè néih heui	give you a ride
M̀ sái la.	That's not necessary.
sàn	new
saigaai	world
jáudim	hotel
Gáulùhng	Kowloon
dīksí	cab
m̀sái	not necessary
gam	so
haakhei	polite
M̀ sái gam haakhei.	No need to do that!
chéng	invite

sìn   in advance

bātgwo   but; however

géisí; géisìh   when

SENTENCE PATTERNS

1. **(Néih) heui bīnsyu a?**
   Where are you going?

2. **(Ngóh) heui hòi sàangyaht pātìh.**
   I'm going to a birthday party.

3. **Kéuih jyuh bīndouh a?**
   Where does he live?

4. **Kéuih jyuh Gáulùhng Sàn Saigaai jáudim.**
   He's staying at the New World Hotel in Kowloon.

5. **Néih géisí sàangyaht a?**
   When is your birthday?

6. **Ngóh gáu yuht sahp ńgh sàangyaht.**
   My birthday is September 15th.

GRAMMAR NOTES

1. When describing the manner of doing something as *"I'll go by taxi,"* *"I will go to Hong Kong by plane,"* *" I'll go to Canton by train,"* it is necessary to use the word *"daap."* It is used with the noun *(taxi, plane, train)* and precedes the verb. For example:

   a) Ngóh daap dīksí heui.

   I'll go by taxi.

   b) Ngóh daap fèigèi heui Náu Yeuk.

   I'll go to New York by airplane.

   c) Kúeih daap fóchè heui Hèunggóng.

   He'll go to Hong Kong by train.

2. Native Cantonese speakers often omit the pronouns *"I"* and *"you"* as a subject in conversation.

   a)   (Néih) heui bīnsyu a?

   Where are you going?

   b)   Heui séjihlàuh.

   I'm going to the office.

3. In Cantonese, the use of the verb *"to give"* *(béi)* is different from English. In English we say *"I give you an apple"*. *"Apple"* is the indirect object. But in Cantonese the sentence would read:

   I give an apple to you.

   Ngóh béi go pìhnggwó néih.

"Béi" is also used as the English preposition *" for"* as in *"I'll buy a gift for you."*

Ngóh máaih gih láihmaht béi néih.

I'll buy a gift to give to you.

TRANSLATION

去生日派對　　Heui Sáangyaht Pātìh

A. 喂，去邊處呀？

拎住一大包禮物。

B. 去開生日派對。

A. 邊個生日呀？

B. 我嘅美國朋友保羅，舊年我哋一齊做事。

A. 佢住邊度呀？

我車你去啦！

B. 唔使啦！

佢住九龍新世界酒店。我搭的士去得啦！

A. 咁客氣。你幾時生日呀？到時我送件禮物比你啦！

B. 我九月十五生日，不過唔使咁客氣啦！到時我會請你嚟我
嘅生日派對。

A. 多謝你先。拜拜！

Jiht Dīksí

Catching a Cab

A. Wai, dīksí!	Hey, taxi!
B. Heui bīndouh a?	Where are you going?
A. Gáulùhng Sàn Saigaai jáudim.	New World Hotel in Kowloon.
B. M̀heui, gódouh hóu sākchè ga.	I don't want to go, there's always a traffic jam there.

* * *   * * *

A. Wai, dīksí!	Hey, taxi!
C. Heui bīnsyu a?	Where are you going?
A. Gáulùhng Sàn Saigaai jáudim.	New World Hotel in Kowloon.

C. Deuim̀hjyuh, m̀heui
Gáulùhng.

Sorry, I don't go to Kowloon.

A. Yáuh móuh gáaucho a.

You're kidding!

* * *

A. Wai, dīksí!

Hey, taxi!

D. M̀ heui a. Gau jūng sāugùng
la!

Sorry, it's quitting time!

A. Yáuh móuh gáaucho a.

You're kidding!

* * *   * * *

A. Wai, dīksí!

Hey, taxi!

E. Heui bīndouh a?

Where are you going?

A. M̀ gòi, dáng ngóh séuhngjó
chè sìn góng. Ngóh yáuh
gāpsih a. Ngóh béi dòdī tīpsí
néih.

Let me get in before I tell you. I'm
in a hurry. I will give you a big tip!

E. Yáuh móuh gáaucho a? Síujé,
néih heui bīndouh a?

Are you kidding? Miss, where are
you going?

A. Gáulùhng Sàn Saigaai
jáudim. M̀ gòi néih lā. Sàam
ga dīksí dōu m̀heui a.

New World Hotel in Kowloon.
Please do me this favor. Three cabs
have refused to go.

E. **Hóu lā, ngóh chè néih heui.**
Gin néih haih go leng néui.

Okay. I'll take you because you are a pretty girl.

VOCABULARY

gódouh	there
sākchè	traffic jam
Yáuh móuh gáaucho a.	You're kidding!
gau jūng sāugùng	quitting time
séuhng chè	get in
yáuh gāpsih	in a hurry
tīpsī	tip
dòdī	more
m̀heui	don't go
leng	pretty
néui jái	girl

SENTENCE PATTERNS

1. **Ṁheui, gódouh hóu sākchè ga.**
   I don't want to go, there's always a traffic jam there.

2. **Gau jūng sāugùng la!**
   Sorry, it's quitting time!

3. **Dáng ngóh séuhngjó chè sìn góng.**
   Let me get in before I tell you.

GRAMMAR NOTES

1. In Chinese the order in which an address is given is the reverse of English. Chinese goes from *big to small*, i.e., country, state or province, street name, house number, floor or room number.

   a) **Hèunggóng Gáulùhng Jordan douh**

   155 houh sàam láu, A-3

   155 Jordan St. 3rd Floor #A-3

   Kowloon, Hong Kong

b) Jùnggwok Gwóngdùng Gwóngjàu

Jùngsàan Yih Louh   25 houh sei láu

25 Zhongshan 2nd Road 4th Floor

Guangdong, Guangzhou, China

2. The ordinal numbers in Cantonese are formed by adding **"Daih"** to the cardinal numbers. For example:

a) **yāt**	*(one)*	<u>daih</u> **yāt**	*(first)*
b) **yih**	*(two)*	<u>daih</u> **yih**	*(second)*
c) **yihsahp**	*(twenty)*	<u>daih</u> **yihsahp**	*(twentieth)*
d) **sàamsahp sei**		<u>daih</u> **sàmmsahp sei**	
	(thirty four)		*(thirty fourth)*
e) **luhk**	*(six)*	<u>daih</u> **luhk**	*(thirty sixth)*

3. When expressing numbers of building floors, cardinal numbers are used instead of ordinals.

Yāt	**láu**	*First Floor*
Yih	**láu**	*Second Floor*
Sàam	**láu**	*Third Floor*

Ngóh jyuh hái Gáulùhng Gwóngbo douh baatsahp ngh houh baat láu.

I live on the eighth floor, Eighty Five Broadcast Drive, Kowloon.

TRANSLATION

截的士　　Jiht Dīksí

A. 喂，的士！

B. 去邊度呀？

A. 九龍新世界酒店。

B. 唔去，個道好塞車㗎。

A. 喂，的士！

C. 去邊處呀？

A. 九龍新世界酒店。

C. 對唔住，唔去九龍。

A. 有冇搞錯呀……

A. 喂，的士！

D. 唔去呀，夠鍾收工啦！

A. 有冇搞錯呀……

A. 喂，的士！

E. 去邊度？

A. 唔該，等我上咗車先講啦！

我有急事！

我比多啲貼士你！

E. 有冇搞錯呀？

小姐，你去邊度呀？

A. 九龍新世界酒店。

唔該你啦！三架的士都唔去呀！

E. 好啦！我車你去！

見你係個靚女！

UNIT 13

Hái Dím Sàm Chàh Làuh
At a Dim Sum Restaurant

A. Chéngmahn, géiwái a?
Excuse me, how many in your party?

B. Léuhng wái.
Two.

A. Chéng gàn ngóh làih lā.
Follow me, please!

C. Chéngmahn, yám mātyéh chàh?
Excuse me, what kind of tea would you like?

B. Hèungpín. M̀ gòi, béi būi bīngséui.
Jasmine tea and ice water, please!

C. Yiu dī mātyéh sihk a? Yáuh hàgáau, sìumáai, chàsìubàau tùhng ngàuyuhkyún.
What would you like? We have steamed shrimp dumplings, steamed pork dumplings, steamed barbequed pork bun and beef meatballs.

B. Yāt yéung yāt lùhng lā. Sihk la, m̀hóu haakhei a.

One of each, please. Help yourself!

D. Nīdī haih mātyét ?

What are these?

C. Fuhnjáau, fuhnjáau jīkhaih gāigeuk.

"Fuhnjáau," fuhnjáau means chicken feet.

D. M̀ haih gwa? "Gāigeuk?" Ngóh m̀sihk gāigeuk. Būtyìh giu dihp gòncháau ngàuhhó lā.

No kidding! Chicken feet? I don't eat chicken feet. How about fried rice noodles with beef?

C. Cháau fán hóu m̀hóu sihk a?

How do you like the fried rice noodles?

D. Hóu, jànhaih hóu sihk.

Good. It's really good!

B. Juhng yiu dī mātyéh tìm a?

Would you like something else?

D. Hóu báau la, dòjehsaai néih.

No, thank you. I'm full.

B. Fógei, m̀gòi, màaihdāan.

Waiter, bring me the bill, please!

C. Jáu làh? Chéng heui gwaihmín jáausou. Dòjehsaai.

Are you leaving? Please pay at the counter. Thank you very much.

B. M̀ gòi.

Thank you.

VOCABULARY

géiwái	how many people
léuhng	two (with measure word)
gàn ngóh làih	follow me
hèungpín	jasmine tea
hàgáau	steamed shrimp dumpling
sìumáai	steamed barbequed pork dumpling
chàsìubàau	steamed pork bun
ngàuyuhkyún	beef ball
yāt yéung yāt lùhng	one of each
fuhnjáau	chicken feet
gòncháau ngàuhhó	fried rice noodles with beef
Būtyìh . . .	How about . . .
fán	rice noodle
báau	full

fógei	waiter
Màaihdāan!	Bring me the bill.
jáu	leave
gwaihmín	counter
jáausou	pay the cashier

SUPPLEMENTARY WORDS

chēungyún	fried spring rolls
chàsìu chéungfán	steamed rice flour rolls with barbecued pork
sihjàp pàaihgwàt	steamed spareribs with soy bean sauce
yeuhng chèngjìu	stuffed green pepper with fish
yeuhng ngáigwà	stuffed egg plant with minced pork
hòuhyàuh gaailáan	Chinese broccoli in oyster sauce
ja yeuhng háaihkìhm	deep fried crab claws
wòtip	pot stickers
daahntāat	egg custard

SENTENCE PATTERNS

1. **M̀gòi, béi būi bīngséui.**
   Give me ice water, please!

2. **Sihk lā, m̀hóu haakhei a.**
   Help yourself!

3. **Būtyìh giu dihp gòncháau ngàuhhó lā.**
   How about fried rice noodles with beef?

4. **Cháau fán hóu m̀hóu sihk a?**
   How do you like the fried rice noodles?

5. **Fógei, m̀gòi, màaidāan.**
   Waiter, bring me the bill, please!

6. **Jáu la? Chéng heui gwaihmín jáausou.**
   Are you leaving? Please pay at the counter.

GRAMMAR NOTES

1. In Lesson 9 we introduced the pattern:

    M̀gòi, béi *(give)* **+ Measure Word + Noun** *(food)*

    When ordering dim sum, the following sentence patterns should be used:

    a.   **M̀gòi, béi yāt _go_ chàsìubàau.**

    May I have one steamed barbecued pork bun?

    (Take out food.)

    b.   **M̀gòi, béi léuhng _lòhng_ ngàuhyuhkyún.**

    Please give me two orders of beef meatballs.

    (To be used in a dim sum restaurant.)

    Note: In a dim sum restaurant most of the food is brought in bamboo baskets which are used in the steaming process.The word for *"bamboo basket"* is **"lòhng"** and is used as a measure word as illustrated above.

2. **"Noun + hóu m̀hóu + verb"** means *"How do you like...?"*

    a.   **Cháau fán hóu m̀hóu sihk a?**

    How do you like the fried rice noodles?

    b.   **Dihnyíng hóu m̀hou tái a?**

    Did you like the movie?

3. **"Hóu"** means *" good", "yes"* and **"m̀hóu"** is the *negative "not good"* or *"no."* When combined with a verb as in **"hóu m̀hóu +verb"** the meaning is changed to *"How do you like...?"*

a. **_Cháau fán_ hóu m̀hóu _sihk_ a?**

(Literally - *"Fried rice noodles good/not good to eat?"*)

How do you like fried rice noodles?

b. **_Dihnyíng_ hóu m̀hóu _tái_ a?**

(Literally - *"the movie good/not good to watch?"*)

Did you like the movie?

TRANSLATION

喺點心茶樓　Hái Dím Sàm Chàh Làuh

A. 請問，幾位呀？

B. 兩位。

A. 請跟我嚟啦！

C. 請問，飲乜嘢茶？

B. 香片。

　　唔該，比杯冰水。

C. 要啲乜嘢食呀？

　　有蝦餃，燒賣，叉燒包同牛肉丸。

B. 一樣一籠啦！

　　食啦！唔好客氣呀！

D. 呢啲係乜嘢？

C. "鳳爪"，鳳爪即係雞腳。

D. 唔係呱？"雞腳"？

　　我唔食雞腳！

　　不而叫碟乾炒牛河啦！

C. 炒粉好唔好食呀？

D. 好，眞係好食。

B. 重要啲乜嘢添呀！

D. 好飽了，多謝晒你！

B. 伙計，唔該，埋單！

C. 走啦？

　　請去櫃面找數。

　　多謝晒！

B. 唔該！

UNIT **14**

Jāumuht
Weekend Activities

**A. Néih láihbaaihyaht
tūngsèuhng jouh mātyéh?**

What do you usually do on
Sundays?

**B. Hái ngūkkéi táisyù waahkjé
táidihnsih. Yáuhsìh heui
gùngyún saanbouh waakjé
heui taam pàhngyáuh. Néih
nē?**

I usually read or watch TV at home.
Sometimes I go to the park for a
walk or go visit friends. How about
you?

**A. Ngóh dōsou heui táidihnyíng
waahkjé táidábō. Yáuhsìh
ngóhdeih heui ngoihbihn
sihkfaahn.**

Most of the time I go to the movies
or watch ballgames. Sometimes we
go out to eat.

**B. Néih taaitáai jùng m̀jùngyi
heui hàahng gùngsì?**

Does your wife like window
shopping?

135

A. Kéuih hóusíu heui hàahng gùngsì. Kéuih jùngyi heui gāaisíh máaihsung, chéng chānchìk pàhngyáuh làih ngūkkéi sihkfaahn.

No, she seldom window shops. She likes to go to the market to shop for groceries. Then we have relatives and friends come over for dinner.

B. Ngóh taaitáai sìhsìh heui hàahnggāai máaihyéh, máahnhāak tùhng chānchìk "bòudihnwájùk."

My wife often goes shopping. In the evenings she likes to talk on the telephone to relatives.

A. Haih mē? Néihdeih tìngyaht m̀sái fàangùng, ngóhdeih chéng néih tùhng néih taaitáai heui sihkfaahn, yìnhauh yātchàih heui tèng gō, hóu ma?

Is that so? Since you don't have to go to work tomorrow, we would like to invite you and your wife to go out to dinner and a show. O.K.?

B. Dòjeh néihdeih sìn. Dáng ngóh mahnháh ngóh lóuhpòh, yihnhauh joi dádihnwá béi néih lā.

Thank you in advance. Let me ask my wife and then I will call you.

A. O.K. Bāaibaai.

Okay. Bye-bye.

VOCABULARY

láihbaaihyaht	Sunday
tūngsèuhng	usually
jouh	do
táidihnsih	watch TV
táisyù	read (book)
waahkjé	or
gùngyún	park
saanbouh	walk
taam	visit (people)
dōsou	most of the time
táidihnyíng	go to a movie
táidábō	ballgame
ngoihbihn	outside
sihkfaahn	have dinner

hàahng gùngsì	window shopping
hóusíu	seldom
gāaisíh	market
máaihsung	shop for groceries
chānchìk	relative
sìhsìh	often
máahnhāak	in the evening
"bòudihnwájùk"	talk on the telephone
Haih mē?	Is that so?
tìngyaht	tomorrow
m̀sái fàangùng	don't have to go to work
tèng gō	a show
mahn	ask

SENTENCE PATTERNS

1. **Néih láihbaaihyaht tūngsèuhng jouh mātyéh?**
   What do you usually do on Sundays?

2. **(Ngóh) hái ngūkkéi táisyù waahkjé táidihnsih.**
   I usually read or watch TV at home.

3. **Ngóh taaitáai kéuih hóusíu heui hàahng gùngsì.**
   My wife seldom window shops.

4. **Kéuih tìngyaht yiu heui máaihyéh.**
   She will go shopping tomorrow.

5. **Ngóh tìngyaht m̀sái fàangùng.**
   I don't have to work tomorrow.

GRAMMAR NOTES

1. There is no future tense in Cantonese. The action in the future is indicated by a future time word. But when the "need" of the future action is emphasized, **"yiu"** *(need)* or **"wúih"** *(will)* is used. Compare:

   a. **Ngóh taaitáai tìngyaht yiu heui máaihyéh.**

   My wife tomorrow will need to go shopping.

> **b.**   **Kéuih tìngyaht wúih dá dihnwá béi néih.**
>
> She will call you tomorrow.

2. For negative statements of future action, **"m̀ + verb"** is used; **m̀sái + verb"** means *"don't have to."*

   Compare:

   a)   **Ngóh tìngyaht m̀heui máaihyéh.**

   I won't go shopping tomorrow.

   b)   **Ngóh tìngyaht m̀sái heui máaihyéh. Ngóh taaitáai heui.**

   I don't have to go shopping tomorrow. My wife will go.

TRANSLATION

周末   Jāumuht

A. 你禮拜日通常做乜嘢？

B. 喺屋企睇書或者睇電視。

有時去公園散步或者去探朋友。你呢？

A. 我多數去睇電影或者睇打波。

有時我哋去外面食飯。

B. 你太太中唔中意去行公司？

A. 佢好少去行公司。佢中意去街市買餸，請親戚朋友嚟屋企食飯。

B. 我太太時時去行街買嘢，晚黑同親戚 "煲電話粥"。

A. 係咩？

你哋聽日唔使返工，我哋請你同你太太去食飯，然後一齊去聽歌，好嗎？

B. 多謝你哋先。

等我問下我老婆，然後再打電話俾你啦！

A. O.K. 。拜拜！

Dá Sīyàhn Dihnwa

A Personal Telephone Call

C. Wái. Bīnwái a?

Hello, who is this?

A. M̀ gòi, Jèung sìnsàang hái ngūkkéi ma?

Is Mr. Jung at home?

C. Hái a. Chéngmahn gwaising wán kéuih?

Yes. May I ask who's calling?

A. Síu sing Chàhn.

My last name is Chan.

C. Chàhn sìnsàang, chéng dángyātjahn. Lóuhgùng, tèng dihnwá. Sing Chàhn ge dá làih ga.

Mr. Chan, hold on, please! (Calls to husband.) Honey, a call for you. It's Mr. Chan.

B. Wái, Chàhnsàang. Ngóh kàhmmáahn dágwo dihnwá béi néih, néihdeih móuh yàhn hái ngūkkéi.

Hello, Mr. Chan. I called you yesterday evening. There was nobody at home.

A. Haih a, ngóh tùhng lóuhpòh
heuijó gèichèuhng jip
chānchìk.
Tìngmáahn yātchàih heui
sihkfaahn tùhng téng gō.
Móuh mahntàih ma?

That's right. My wife and I went to
the airport to meet relatives. Is
there any problem with us going out
to dinner and a show?

B. Yáuh mahntàih a! Ngóh
taaitáai yeukjó pàhngyáuh
heui máaihyéh, būtyìh hahgo
láihbaaihyaht lā. Ngóhdeih
chéng néihdeih lā.

Yes, there is a problem. My wife
made plans to go shopping with a
friend. Can we take you out next
Sunday?

A. Bīngo chéng dōu yātyeuhng
lā. Ngóh séung néih taaitáai
tùhng ngóh taaitáai yihnsīk
yihngsīk.

We'll worry about who pays for it
later. I just want our wives to meet
each other.

B. Hóu, móuh mahntàih, hahgo
láihbaaiyaht gin la.

Good. No problem. See you next
Sunday.

VOCABULARY

hái	at, in, on
síu sing	last name (humble way)
chéng dángyātjahn; chéng dángdáng	hold on
lóuhgùng; lóuhpòh	honey (husband, wife)
tèng dihnwá	a call for you
kàhmmáahn	yesterday evening
dágwo	called
heuijó	went
gèichèuhng	airport
jip	meet
mahntàih	problem
heui máaihyéh	go shopping
Bīngo chéng dōu yātyeuhng lā.	We'll worry about who pays for it later.

yihnsīk   to know each other

Móuh mahntàih!   No problem!

hahgo láihbaaihyaht   next Sunday

SENTENCE PATTERNS

1. **Ngóh kàhmmáahn dágwo dihnwá béi néih, néihdeih móuh yàhn hái ngūkkéi.**
   I called you yesterday evening. There was nobody at home.

2. **Ngóh tùhng taaitáai heuijó gèichèuhng jip chānchìk.**
   My wife and I went to the airport to meet relatives.

3. **Hahgo láihbaaiyaht gin la.**
   See you next Sunday.

LET'S TALK CANTONESE

GRAMMAR NOTES

1. Past tense

"-Gwo" when added to a verb indicates past tense.

Ngóh kàhmmáahn dágwo dihnwá béi néih.

I called you yesterday evening.

2. Present perfect tense

"-Jó" when added to a verb indicates an action which has been completed. In American English it is usually translated as a past tense.

Ngóh tùhng taaitáai heuijó gèichèuhng jip chānchìk.

My wife and I went to the airport to meet relatives.

To form a question in the present perfect tense the question particle *"meih"* is used at the ned of the sentence.

1) **a) Kéuih heuijó fàan gùng.**

She went to work.

b) Kéuih heuijó fàan gùng meih?

Did she go to work?

2) **a) Ngóh sihkjó ngaanjau la.**

I have had lunch.

b) Néih sihkjó ngaanjau meih?

Have you had lunch?

To anser the question:

Sihkjó la.

Yes, I did.

Meih.   (*or:* **Meih sihk.**)

No, I didn't.

3. Future tense

There is no future tense in Cantonese. The future is conveyed by the words for *"tomorrow" "next year" etc.* To contrast present tense and future tense are the following examples:

Ngóh yaht yaht dá dinhwá béi néih.

I call you everyday.

(I everyday call for you.)

Ngóh tìngyaht dá dinhwá béi néih.

I'll call you tomorrow.

(I tomorrow call for you.)

Ngóhdeih chēutnín heui Hèunggóng.

We'll go to Hong Kong next year.

(We'll next year go Hong Kong.)

Please note the placement of the time word *(tomorrow, next year)* after the subject.

TRANSLATION

打（私人）電話　　Dá Sīyàhn Dihnwá

C. 喂，邊位呀？

A. 唔該，張先生喺屋企嗎？

C. 喺，請問貴姓搵佢？

A. 小姓陳。

C. 陳先生，請等一陣。

　　老公，聽電話，姓陳嘅打嚟！

B. 喂，陳生！我噚晚打過電話比你，你冇人喺屋企。

A. 係，我同老婆去咗機場接親戚。

　　嚦晚一齊去食飯同聽歌。冇問題嗎？

B. 有問題呀。我太太約咗朋友去買嘢，不而下個禮拜日啦，

　　我哋請你哋啦！

A. 邊個請都一樣啦！

　　我想你太太同我太太認識認識！

B. 好，冇問題，下禮拜日見啦！

Dá Sèungyihp Dihnwa
A Business Telephone Call

A. Jóusàhn, Gàm Bóu Yèuhng Hóng.

Good morning. Gàm Bóu Company.

B. M̀ gòi, giu Johnson sìnsàang tèng dihnwá.

Excuse me, Mr. Johnson, please!

A. Kéuih gónggán dihnwá, chéngmahn bīnwái wán kéuih?

He is talking on the telephone right now. May I ask who's calling, please?

B. Ngóh yātjahn joi dá làih lā. M̀ gòi.

I will call back. Thank you.

* * *

A. Jóusàhn, Gàm Bóu Yèuhng Hóng.

Good morning. Gàm Bóu Company.

C. M̀ gòi, Chàhn gìngléih

May I speak to Manager (Mr.)

háidouh ma? Ngóh haih Hàhng sàng ngàhnhòhng sing Léih ge.	Chan? I am Lee from Hang Seng Bank.
A. Chàhn gìngléih hòigán wúi, Chéngmahn yáuh mātyéh sih?	Manager Chan is in a meeting. May I take a message?
C. Chéng giu kéuih dá dihnwá béi ngóh.	Please ask him to call me back.
A. Hóu, néih haih Hàhng sàng ngàhnhòhng ge Léih sìnsàang. Bāaibaai.	Okay. You are Mr. Lee from Hang Seng Bank. Bye-bye.

* * *

A. Jóusàhn, Gàm Bóu Yèuhng Hóng.	Good morning. Gàm Bóu Company.
B. M̀gòi, Johnson sìnsàang dākhàahn ma?	Excuse me, is Mr. Johnson available?
A. Kéuih juhng gónggán dihnwá bo. Yáuh mātyéh sih chéng wahdài la.	He is still talking on the phone. Can I take a message?
B. Chéng néih wah béi kéuih tèng, ngóh gàmyaht hahjau sàam dím làih wán kéuih. Ngóh sing Wān.	Please tell him I'm coming to see him at 3:00 this afternoon. My last name is Wan.

A. Hóu, ngóh wúih wah keuih
   tèng la, Wān Sàang.
   Bāaibaai.

Okay. I will tell him, Mr. Wan.
Bye-bye.

VOCABULARY

yèuhng hóng	foreign company
gónggán	is talking
joi dá làih	call back
gìngléih	manager
Hàhng sàng ngàhnhòhng	Hang Seng Bank
dākhàahn	available
Yáuh mātyéh sih chéng wahdài la.	Can I take a message?
wah	tell
wúih	will

SENTENCE PATTERNS

1. **M̀gòi, giu Johnson sìnsàang tèng dihnwá.**
   Excuse me, Mr. Johnson, please!

2. **Kéuih gónggán dihnwá.**
   He is talking on the telephone right now.

3. **Chéngmahn bīnwái wán kéuih?**
   May I ask who's calling, please?

4. **Chéng giu kéuih dá dihnwá béi ngóh.**
   Please ask him to call me back.

5. **Chéng néih wah béi kéuih tèng, ngóh gàmyaht hahjau sàam dím làih wán kéuih.**
   Please tell him I'm coming to see him at 3:00 this afternoon.

GRAMMAR NOTES

1. **"Giu"** has two meanings:

    a)   *"ask"* somebody to do something

    Ṁgòi, _giu_ Johnson sìngsàang tèng dihnwá!

    Excuse me, please ask Mr. Johnson to answer the phone!

    Chéng _giu_ kéuih dá dihnwá béi ngóh!

    Please ask him to call me back!

    b)   *"be called"*

    Néih _giu_ mātyéh méng a?

    (Literally - *You are called by what name?*)

    What's your name?

    Ngóh _giu_ Méih Lìhng.

    I'm called Mei Ling.

2. **"-gán"** is a verbal suffix which shows action occurring now, that is, continuous tense.

    a)   **Kéuih máahn máahn dōu _tái_ dihnsih.**

    He watches television every night.

    Kéui yìhgā _táigán_ dihnsih.

    He is watching television now.

    b)   **Kéuih góng_gán_ dihnwá.**

    He is talking on the phone right now.

3. The phrase "tell him that..." followed by an object clause is composed by using the verb **"wah"** (to tell) as follows: **"wah béi kéuih tèng."**

   a) **Chéng néih _wah béi kéuih tèng_, ngóh gàmmáahn làih wán kéuih.**

   *Please tell him **that** I'll come to see him tonight.*

   b) **Ngóh bōsí <u>wah béi ngóh tèng</u>, néih dāgwo dihnwá béi ngóh.**

   *My boss told me **that** you called me.*

4. In summary:

   Góng *to speak, to talk , to say*

   Wah *to tell*

   giu *to be called, ask somebody to do something*

TRANSLATION

打商業電話　　Dá Sèungyihp Dihnwá

A. 早晨，金寶洋行。

B. 唔該，叫莊晨先生聽電話。

A. 佢講緊電話，請問邊位搵佢？

B. 我一陣再打嚟啦！

　　唔該！

A. 早晨，金寶洋行。

C. 唔該，陳經理喺道嗎？我係恆生銀行姓李嘅。

A. 陳經理開緊會，請問有乜嘢事？

C. 請叫佢打電話俾我。

A. 好，你係恆生銀行李先生。拜拜！

A. 早晨，金寶洋行。

B. 唔該，莊晨先生得閒嗎？

A. 佢重講緊電話播。

有乜嘢事請話低啦！

B. 請你話比佢聽，我今日下晝三點嚟搵佢。

我姓溫。

A. 好，我會話佢聽啦，溫生。

拜拜！

UNIT 17

Tìnhei

Weather

A. Wah, Hèunggóng jànhaih géi yiht. Gàmyaht géi douh?	Whew! It's really hot in Hong Kong. What's the temperature today?
B. Sàam sahp sei sipsih douh. Kàhmyaht sàam sahp ngh douh, yihtgwo gàmyaht.	Thirty four degrees Centigrade. And yesterday was thirty five. It was hotter than today.
A. Tìngyaht nē?	How about tomorrow?
B. Tìnhei bougou wah tìngyaht wúih juhng yiht - sàam sahp luhk douh.	The weather report says that tomorrow it will get even hotter -- thirty six degrees.
A. Wah, m̀haih gwa! Sàam sahp luhk douh!	Whew! No kidding! Thirty six degrees?
B. Hèunggóng jeui yiht haih chāt yuht tùhng baat yuht. Bātgwo gàmmáahn wúih	July and August are the hottest months in Hong Kong. However, it will rain tonight.

lohkyúh.

A. **Gám jauh wúih lèuhngdī la.** So it will get cooler.

B. **Haih. Néihdeih** Is it this hot in the summer in San
Sàamfàahnsíh hahtìn yáuh Francisco?
móuh gáhm yiht?

A. **Móuh, Sàamfàahnsíh hahtìn** No. The summer in San Francisco
haih hóu láahng ga. is cold.

B. **M̀ haih gwa! Hóu láahng?** No kidding! Cold? What are the
Géidō douh a? temperatures?

A. **Luhk sahp dou chāt sahp** From 60 to 70 degrees Fahrenheit
douh wàhsih, jìk haih sahp or 16 to 21 degrees Centigrade.
luhk dou yih sahp yāt douh
sipsih.

B. **Dūngtìn nē? Lohk** How about in winter? Does it
m̀lohksyut? snow?

A. **M̀ lohk. Yāt nìhn seigwai dōu** No, it doesn't. It's mild all year
m̀láahng m̀yiht, bātgwo round. But it's usually windy.
sìhsìh dōu yáuh fùng.

B. **Gám jauh jànhaih hóu la.** Oh, that's really good.

VOCABULARY

Wah!	Whew!
Hèunggóng	Hong Kong
géi; hóu	very
yiht	hot
gàmyaht	today
kàhmyaht	yesterday
douh	degree
sipsih	Centigrade
yihtgwo	hotter than
tìnhei	weather
bougou	report
wah	say
juhng	even
jeui yiht	hottest

yuht	month
bātgwo	however
gàmmáahn	tonight
lohkyúh	rain
lèuhngdī	cooler
gáhm yiht	this hot
láahng	cold
wàhsih	Fahrenheit
dūngtìn	winter
seigwai	four seasons
lohksyut	snow
m̀láahng m̀yiht	mild (not cold, not hot)
yáuh fùng	windy

SENTENCE PATTERNS

1. **Hèunggóng jànhaih géi yiht.**
   It's really hot in Hong Kong.

2. **Kàhmyaht yihtgwo gàmyaht.**
   Yesterday was hotter than today.

3. **Tìngyaht wúih juhng yiht.**
   Tomorrow will get even hotter.

4. **Hèunggóng jeui yiht haih chāt yuht tùhng baat yuht.**
   July and August are the hottest months in Hong Kong.

GRAMMAR NOTES

1. To form comparatives such as *"bigger than,"* the suffix **"-gwo"** is added to the adjective.

A hóu daaih.	*A is very big.*
B daaih<u>gwo</u> A.	*B is bigger than A.*
C juhng daaih<u>gwo</u> B.	*C is even bigger than B.*
D <u>jeui</u> daaih.	*D is the biggest of the four.*

   Note: a) The verb *"to be"* **(haih)** is not needed in the above structure.

b) **"Jeui"** + adjective shows the superlative.

2. Following are some frequently used adjectives and their antonyms for practicing comparatives:

Adjective + gwo

yiht	*(hot)*	**láahng**	*(cold)*
daaih	*(big)*	**sai**	*(small)*
chèuhng	*(long)*	**dyún**	*(short in length)*
gòu	*(tall)*	**ngái**	*(short in height)*
fèih	*(fat)*	**sau**	*(thin)*
faai	*(fast)*	**maahn**	*(slow)*
lēk	*(smart)*	**chéun**	*(stupid)*
pèhng	*(cheap)*	**gwai**	*(expensive)*
hóu	*(good)*	**chā/séui**	*(bad in quality /personality)*
leng	*(pretty)*	**cháugwaai**	*(ugly)*

TRANSLATION

天氣　　　Tìnhei

A. 嘩，香港眞係幾熱，今日幾度？

B. 34 攝氏度。

噚日 35 度，熱過今日。

A. 嚟日呢？

B. 天氣報告話嚟日會重熱 — 36度。

A. 嘩，唔係呱！

B. 香港最熱係七月同八月。不過今晚會落雨。

A. 咁就會涼啲啦！

B. 係！你哋三藩市夏天有冇咁熱？

A. 冇，三藩市夏天係好冷！

B. 唔係呱？好冷？

幾多度呀？

A. 六十到七十度華氏，即係十三到二十一度攝氏。

B. 冬天呢？落唔落雪？

A. 唔落。

一年四季都唔冷唔熱，不過時時都有風。

B. 咁，就真係好啦！

UNIT 18

Bàbai ge Bōsí

A Demanding Boss

A. **Wòhng síujé, m̀gòi, jàm būi chàh béi ngóh.**
Miss Wong, please pour me a cup of tea.

Wòhng síujé, chéng chùng būi gafē béi Jèung sìnsàang.
Miss Wong, please get a cup of coffee for Mr. Jung.

Wòhng síujé, m̀gòi ló guin hòlohk béi Léih sìnsàang.
Miss Wong, please bring a can of Coke to Mr. Lee.

* * *

A. **Wòhng síujé, ngóh jì bāt hái bīndouh?**
Miss Wong, where's my pen?

B. **Hái gó jèung tói seuhngmihn.**
It's on that table.

A. **M̀gòi, ló jì bāt béi ngóh.**
Please bring the pen to me.

* * *

A. **Wòhng síujé, ngóh dī kāatpín**
Miss Wong, where are my business cards?

hái bīndouh?

B. Hái néihge gùngsihbāau léuihbihn.	They are inside your briefcase.
A. M̀ gòi, ló ngóh ge gùngsihbāau béi ngóh.	Please bring my briefcase to me.

* * *

A. Wòhng síujé, fahn hahptùhng hái bīndouh?	Miss Wong, where's the contract?
B. Hái néih jèung tói jóbihn ge gwaihtúng.	It's in the lefthand drawer of your desk.
A. M̀ gòi, ngóh jihgéi ló la.	Thank you. I'll get it myself.

* * *

A. Wòhng síujé, Jèung sìnsaàng hái bīndouh?	Miss Wong, where is Mr. Jung?
B. Hái wuihaaksāt.	He is in the conference room.
A. M̀ gòi, nīng nī fahn hahptùhng béi kéuih chìmméng.	Please bring this contract to him to sign. Thank you.

* * *

A. Wòhng síujé, Léih sìnsaàng	Miss Wong, where is Mr. Lee?

hái bīndouh?

B. Hái wuihaaksāt.   He is in the conference room.

A. M̀gói, giu kéuih yahplàih.   Please ask him to come here. Thank you.

B. Bōsí, ngóh juhng yáuh móuh sih yiu joh a?   Boss, is there anything else I have to do?

A. Móuh la, chéng chēutheui la.   No. You can leave now.

B. Nígo lóuhsai, jànhaih géi bābai.   Oh, this boss is really demanding.

VOCABULARY

jàm	pour
chùng	to prepare (coffee, tea, etc.)
béi	(give something) to (somebody)
ló	bring
bāt	pen
hái seuhngmihn; hái seuhngbihn	on top of
tói	table; desk

kāatpín	business card
gùngsihbāau	briefcase
léuihbihn; léuihmihn	inside
hahptùhng	contract
jóbihn	lefthand
gwaihtúng	drawer
jihgēi	myself
hái bīndouh	where
wuihaaksāt	conference room
chìmméng	sign
yahplàih	come in
chēutheui	leave (Get out!)
bōsí; lóuhsai	boss
bābai	demanding

SENTENCE PATTERNS

1. **Ló jì bāt béi ngóh.**
   Please bring the pen to me.

2. **Néih dī kāatpín hái néihge gùngsihbāau léuihbihn.**
   Your cards are inside your briefcase.

3. **M̀ gói, giu kéuih yahplàih.**
   Please ask him to come here.

4. **Ngóh juhng yáuh móuh sih yiu joh a?**
   Is there anything else I have to do?

GRAMMAR NOTES

1. As we mentioned in Unit 4, most nouns in Cantonese use measure words, i.e.

yāt jì bāt	*a pen*
yāt go gùnsihbāau	*a briefcase*
yāt būi gafē	*a cup of coffee*

Note, however, that in a sentence such as *"Bring me a pen,"* the word **"yāt"** (one) is omitted. The pattern would then read **"bring + measure word + noun + for me."**

Ló jì bāt béi ngóh.

Bring me a pen.

For more than one item the number is used before the measure word:

Ló sàam jì bāt béi ngóh.

Bring me three pens.

Where the noun for the item is plural, the measure word **"dī"** is used.

Ló dī kāatpín béi ngóh.

Bring me some business cards.

"Seuhngbihn" *(on top of)* , **"léuihbihn"** *(*inside), **"jóbihn"** *(on the left)* and **"yauhmihn"** *(on the right)* are place words which function like nouns in Cantonese instead of prepositions or prepositional phrases in English. Compare:

tói seuhngbihn	*on the table*
gùngsihbāau leuihbihn	*inside the briefcase*
tói jóbihn	*on the left of the table*

Using nouns to modify nouns is a very common structure in Cantonese. In the phrase **tói seuhngbihn,** **"tói"** is a noun modifying **"seuhngbihn"** and functions as an attribute.

As an example, "The Bank of America in San Francisco" would literally translate to Cantonese as "San Francisco America Bank," where "San Francisco" and "America" modify the noun "Bank." It looks like this in Cantonese:

Sàamfaàhsíh Méihgwok Ngàhnhòhng

All attributes in Cantonese precede the noun they modify. This presents a difficulty for English speakers because in English attributes can either precede the noun they modify or succeed the noun. To illustrate:

<u>my</u> <u>red</u> pen <u>on the table</u> of <u>my boss...</u>

1   2   3   4

Numbers 1, 2, 3, and 4 are attributes modifying pen.

In Cantonese the phrase would be structured as:

<u>my boss</u> <u>on the table</u> <u>my</u> <u>red</u> pen

4   3   1   2

Ngóh gó jì hái ngóh bōsí tói seuhngbihn ge hòhng <u>bāt</u>

Since there is no easy way to learn this concept, we suggest that the learner read the dialogue again and again to acquire the rule.

TRANSLATION

巴閉嘅波士　　**Bábai ge Bōsí**

A.　王小姐，唔該，斟杯茶俾我。

王小姐，請冲杯咖啡俾張先生。

王小姐，唔該攞罐可樂俾李先生。

A.　王小姐，我支筆喺邊度？

B.　喺嗰張檯上面。

A. 唔該，攞支筆俾我。

A. 王小姐，我啲咭片喺邊度？

B. 喺你嘅公事包裡便。

A. 唔該，攞我嘅公事包俾我。

A. 王小姐，份合同喺邊道？

B. 喺你張檯左邊嘅櫃桶。

A. 唔該。我自己攞啦！

A. 王小姐，張先生喺邊度？

B. 喺會客室。

A. 唔該，拎呢份合同俾佢簽名。

A. 王小姐，李先生喺邊度？

B. 喺會客室。

A. 唔該，叫佢入嚟。

B. 波士，我重有冇事要做呀？

A. 冇啦！請出去！

B. 呢個老勢眞係幾巴閉！

Sàngwuht Hái Síh Jùngsàm

Living in the City

A. Ngóh jyuh hái síh jùngsàm ge guhngdouh daaihhah, hóu fòngbihn.

I live in a condominium downtown and it's very convenient.

B. Dím fòngbihn faat a?

Why is it covenient?

A. Daaihhah ge jóbihn haih baakfogùngsì, yauhbihn haih dihnyíngyún, hauhbihn haih chìukāpsíhchèuhng, chìhnbihn haih yàuhgúk.

On the left of the building is a department store and on the right is a movie theater. Behind it is a supermarket and in front of it is a post office.

B. Fuhkahn yáuh móuh jùngchàangún tùhng gùngyún a?

Is there a Chinese restaurant or park nearby?

A. Yáuh, baakfogùnghsì deuimihn haih yāt gāan jùngchāangún,

Yes. Across from the department store is a Chinese restaurant and across from the supermarket is a park.

chìukāpsíhchèuhng deuimihn
jauh haih gùngyún.

B. Gám, yātchai jauh gáaudihmsaai la. Daapchè fòng m̀fòngbihn?	Well, you have almost everything. Is it convenient to take the bus there?
A. Fòngbihn, daaihhah ge deuimihn jauh yáuh bāsí jaahm.	Yes, it is. Across from the building there is a bus station.
B. Daap deihtit fòng m̀fòngbihn?	Is it convenient to take the subway?
A. Fòngbihn, heung chìhn hàahng sàam go gāaiháu jauh haih deihtit jaahm.	It's very convenient. The subway station is three blocks away.
B. Gám jauh jàn haih "móuh-dāk-tàahn" la.	You really do have everything.

VOCABULARY

síh jùngsàm	downtown
guhngdouh daaihhah	condominium
fòngbihn	convenient

dímgáai	why
daaihhah	building
jóbihn	on the left
baakfogùngsì	department store
yauhbihn	on the right
dihnyíngyún	movie theater
hauhbihn	behind
chìukāpsíhchèuhng	supermarket
chìhnbihn	in front of
yàuhgúk	post office
fuhkahn	nearby
jùngchāangún	Chinese restaurant
gùngyún	park
deuimihn	across from
Yātchai jauh gáaudihmsaai la.	You have almost everything.
daapchè	take the bus

bāsí	bus
jaahm	station
deihtit	subway
heung chìhn hàahng	walk down
gāaiháu	block
"Móuhdāk-tàahn"!	Perfect!

SUPPLEMENTARY WORDS

yìyún	hospital
jihkmahtyún	botanical garden
duhngmahtyún	zoo
bokmahtgún	museum
ngaihseuhtgún	museum of art
taaihùnggún	space museum
máhtàuh	pier
tìhngchèchèuhng	parking lot
gāyàuhjaahm	gas station

SENTENCE PATTERNS

1. **Daaihhah ge jóbihn haih baakfogùngsì.**
   On the left of the building is a department store.

2. **Daaihhah ge deuimihn jauh yáuh bāsí jaahm.**
   Across from the building there is a bus station.

3. **Daapchè fòng m̀fòngbihn?**
   Is it convenient to take the bus there?

4. **Heung chìhn hàahng sàam go gāaiháu jauh haih deihtit jaahm.**
   The subway station is three blocks away.

GRAMMAR NOTES

1. As we mentioned in Unit 18, placewords like **"jóbihn"** *(on* the left), **"deuimihn"** *(opposite)* can function as nouns. In sentence patterns 1 and 2 , the place words are the subjects of the sentences.

   Daaihhah ge <u>deuimihn</u> jauh <u>yáuh</u> bāsí jaahm.

   Opposite the building there is a bus station.

Notice that in Cantonese **"yáuh"** means *"to have"* as well as *"there is"* and *"there are."*

2. In sentence pattern 3, we use **"Daapchè fòng m̀fòngbihn?"** *(Is it convenient to take a bus?)* Note that the literal translation is "take a bus convenient or not convenient?" There are two things to remember here. One is the affirmative/negative phrase discussed earlier and the second is the use of **"fòngbihn"** *(convenient.)* Unlike English where *"convenient"* is an adjective, in Cantonese **"fòngbihn"** is called a stative verb which functions as a predicate.

3. Many verb-noun compounds like **"daapchè"** *(take a bus)*, **"jāchè"** (drive a car) and verb phrases like **"hāahng sàam go gāaiháu"** *(walk three blocks)*, **"sàngwuht hái síh jùngsàm** *(living in the city)* can function as subjects (as in the dialogue) or objects, i.e.,

Ngóh jùngyi jāchè.

I like driving.

Ngóh jùngyi sàngwuht hái síh jùngsàm.

I like living in the city.

TRANSLATION

生活喺市中心 Sàngwuht Hái Síh Jùngsàm

A. 我住喺市中心嘅共渡大廈，好方便。

B. 點方便法呀？

A. 大廈嘅左邊係百貨公司,右邊係電影院,後邊係超級市場,前邊係郵局。

B. 附近有冇中餐館同公園呀?

A. 有,百貨公司對面係一間中餐館,超級市場對面就係公園。

B. 咁,一切就搞掂晒啦!

搭車方唔方便?

A. 方便,大廈對面就有巴士站。

B. 搭地鐵方唔方便?

A. 方便,向前行三個街口就係地鐵站。

B. 咁,就真係 " 冇得彈 " 啦!

Mahn Fòngheung

Asking Directions

A. **Chéngmahn, heui "Mùih Sāi"
baakfogùnsì dímyeung
hàahng a?**

Excuse me, how do we get to
Macy's department store?

B. **Hàahng heui?**

Are you going to walk?

A. **Haih a, hóu yúhn àh?**

Yes. Is it far from here?

B. **M̀haih. Yātjihk hàahng sàam
go gāaiháu dou Market gāai
jyún yauh, joi jihk hàahng
léuhng go gāaiháu, joi jyún
yauh, yìhnhauh hái Geary
gāai yātjihk hàahng . . .**

No. Go straight down three blocks
to Market Street, turn right, then
walk two blocks to Geary Street.
Turn right again and walk straight
. . .

A. **Wa, gáhm fūkjaahp, hóuchíh
hóu yúhn bo.**

Wow, that's complicated! It seems
to be very far.

B. **M̀haih hóu yúhn, yùhgwó**

It's not very far from here if you

LET'S TALK CANTONESE

néih sīk louh nē, sahp ńgh
fùnjùng jauh dāk la!

know the way. It only takes you 15
minutes.

A. Yáuh móuh bāsí dou ga?

Does any bus go there?

B. Yáuh, sìn daap sei sahp yih
houh bāsí dou Market gāai
lohkchè, joi jyún sàam sahp
baat houh, jauh dou "Mùih
sāi" gùnsì ge mùhnháu.

Yes. Take the #42 bus to Market
Street and get off then change to the
#38 bus. It will take you right to
Macy's.

A. Yauh haih yiu jyún chè?
Yáuh móuh jihkdaaht chè
ga?

Oh, I need to change buses? Is
there any direct bus?

B. Móuh. Daap dīksí lā. Ńgh
mān dóu jauh gáaudihm la.

No. Take a cab! Five bucks will
get you there.

A. Gám jauh jàn haih bātyìh
daap dīksí la. M̀ gòisaai néih
la.

In that case, I'll take a cab. Thank
you very much.

VOCABULARY

fòngheung	direction
dímyeung	how
hàahng	walk
yúhn	far
yātjihk	straight
jyún	turn
fūkjaahp	complicated
hóuchíh	(it) seem(s)
yùhgwó	if
sīk louh	know the way
fànjùng	minute
yìhnhauh	then
sei sahp yih houh bāsí	#42 bus
gāai	street

lohkchè	get off (bus or train); get out of (car or taxi)
mùhnháu	door
jyún chè	change buses
jihkdaaht	direct
bātyìh	had better

SENTENCE PATTERNS

1. Chéngmahn, heui "Mùih Sāi" baakfogùnsì dímyeung hàahng a?
Excuse me, how do we get to Macy's department store?

2. Yātjihk hàahng sàam go gāaiháu dou Market gāai jyún yauh.
Go straight down three blocks to Market Street, turn right.

3. Yùhgwó néih sīk louh nē, sahp ńgh fùnjùng jauh dāk la.
If you know the way, it only takes you 15 minutes.

4. Daap sei sahp yih houh bāsí dou Market gāai lohkchè.
Take the #42 bus to Market Street and get off at Market Street.

GRAMMAR NOTES

In Cantonese, adverbials or adverbial phrases come before the verb rather than after as in English.

a) **yātjihk <u>hàahng</u>**

down walk

(*walk* down)

b) **Dou Market gāai <u>lohkchè</u>.**

At Market Street get off.

(*Get off* at Market Street.)

TRANSLATION

問方向　　Mahn Fòngheung

A. 請問，去梅西百貨公司點樣行呀？

B. 行去？

A. 係 呀，好遠呀？

B. 唔係，一直行三個街口到孖結大街轉右，又直行兩個街口再轉右，然後喺基理街一直行……

A. 嘩，咁復雜，好似好遠嚙！

B. 唔係好遠，如果你識路呢，十五分鐘就得啦！

A. 有冇巴士到㗎？

B. 有，先搭四十二號巴士到孖結街落車，再轉三十八號，就到梅西公司嘅門口。

A. 又係要轉車？

有冇直達車㗎？

B. 冇。搭的士啦！

五蚊倒就搞掂啦！

A. 咁，就真係不而搭的士啦！

唔該晒你啦！

Jyuh Jáudim

At a Hotel

Dehng Fóng

BOOKING A ROOM

A. Néih hóu. Gayaht jáudim.

Hello, Holiday Inn.

B. M̀ gòi, ngóh dehng yāt go dāanyàhnfóng, jyuh sáam máahn.

Excuse me, I would like to book a single room for three nights.

A. Hóu, chéngmahn bīn yaht dou nē?

Good. May I ask what date you will be arriving?

B. Sìngkèih luhk hahjau, sahp baat houh. Chéngmahn géi chín yāt máahn a?

Saturday afternoon on the 18th. What is your rate?

A. Ngóhdeih ge fóng chùhng múi máahn Góngjí chìn sei héi, dou léuhng chìn yāt máahn.

Our rooms range from HK$1,400 to HK$2,000 per night.

B. Ngóh yiu gàan jeui pèhng ge jauh dāk la.	The cheapest one will be fine.
A. O.K. Chéngmahn gwaising?	Okay. May I ask your last name?
B. Ngóh sing Léih, Léih Wàh.	My last name is Lee, Wa Lee.
A. Chéngmahn dímyeung fuhfún nē?	How would you like to pay?
B. Yuhng Visa seunyuhngkāat.	Visa credit card.
A. Seungyuhngkāat houhmáh.	Credit card number?
B. Sei lìhng yāt baat, lìhng yih yāt yih, sáam luhk gáu chāt .	4018 0212 3697.
A. Sāthaauh kèih.	Expiration date?
B. Gáu ńgh nìhn sahp yuht.	10/95.
A. Dāk la, Léih sìnsàang. Dòjeh néih.	Okay, Mr. Lee. Thank you.

Hái Chìh Tòih	*AT THE FRONT DESK*
B. M̀ gòi, ngóh dehngjó yāt go dāanyàhnfóng, ngóh giu Léih Wàh.	Excuse me, I have a reservation for a single room. My name is Wa Lee.
A. Hóu, chéng tìhn bíu?	Okay. Will you please fill out this form?

B. Nàh, tìhn hóu la.

Here you go. I have filled it out.

A. M̀goì, béi go wuhjiu lèih táiháh. Hóu, gáaudihm la. Néih ge fóng houh haih luhk yāt sàam, go bōi wúih tùhng néih seuhngláu.

Excuse me, may I see your passport? (Looks at it.) Good, you're all set. Your room number is 613. The bellboy will take you to your room.

B. M̀gòi.

Thank you.

Wuhn Fóng

SWITCHING ROOMS

B. M̀hóuyisi, ngóh séung wuhn gàan daaihdī ge fóng.

Excuse me, I would like to change to a bigger room.

A. Deuim̀jyuh, ngóhdeih ge dāanyàhnfóng dōu haih yātyeuhng daaih ga. Yiu tougàan la. Tougàan daaih hóudō, yauh syùfuhk hóudō.

Sorry, all our rooms are the same size. How about a suite? Suites are much bigger and much more comfortable.

B. Wúih m̀wúih gwai hóudō a?

Would that be much more expensive?

A. M̀wúih, tougàan yāt máahn haih léuhng chìn yih, gwai baat baak mān. Ngāam m̀ngāam a?

No, not really. The price for a suite is HK$2,200. Only HK$800 more. Will that be O. K.?

B. Móuh mahntàih, séung syùfuhk jauh yiu sái dōdī chín. Yiu tougàan la.

No problem. More comfort costs more. Let me take the suite.

A. **O.K. Léih sàang, néih ge tougàan fóng houh haih yih yāt sàam yāt. Nàh - béi sósìh néih.**

Okay, Mr. Lee. Your suite number is 2133. Here is your key.

VOCABULARY

dehng fóng	booking a room
gayaht	holiday
jáudim	hotel
dāanyàhnfóng	single room
máahn	night
bīn yaht	what date
dou	arrive
yāt máahn; múi máahn	each night; per night
chùhng . . . dou	from . . . to
múi	per

jeui pèhng	cheapest
fuhfún; béichín	pay
seunyuhngkāat	credit card
houhmáh	number
sāthaauh	expiration
yaht kèih	date
chìh tòih	front desk
tìhn	fill out
bíu	form
wuhjiu	passport
Gáaudihm.	You're all set.
wuhn	change; switch
fóng	room
yātyeuhng daaih	same size
tougàan	suite
syùfuhk	comfortable

hóudō	much more
gwai	expensive
m̀wúih	not really
Móuh mahntàih!	No problem!
sái	spend (money)
sósìh	key

SUPPLEMENTARY WORDS

daaihtòhng	lobby
sàufúnchyúh	cashier
sáisáugāan (chisó)	restroom (toilet)
léuhyàuh bāsí	tourist coach
léuhhahngtyuhn	tour group
hàhngléih	baggage
sìnggonggēi, dihntāi, līp	elevator
chāantāng	restaurant (in a hotel)

SENTENCE PATTERNS

1. **Ngóh dehng yāt go dāanyàhnfóng, jyuh sáam máahn.**
   I would like to book a single room for three nights.

2. **Ngóh yiu gàan jeui pèhng ge jauh dāk la.**
   The cheapest one will be fine.
   (I want the cheapest one.)

3. **Chéngmahn dímyeung fuhfún nē?**
   How would you like to pay?

4. **Ngóh séung wuhn gàan daaihdī ge fóng.**
   I would like to change to a bigger room.

5. **Ngóhdeih ge dāanyàhnfóng dōu haih yātyeuhng daaih ga.**
   Sorry, all our rooms are the same size.

6. **Tougàan daaih hóudō, yauh syùfuhk hóudō.**
   Suites are much bigger and much more comfortable.

GRAMMAR NOTES

1. There are many elliptical sentences in Cantonese conversation. For example:

   a)   **Jyuh sàam máahn.**

   Stay for three nights. (I **"ngóh"** is omitted.)

   b)   **Chéngmahn, dímyeung fuhfún nēi ?**

   May I ask how you will pay? (You **"néih"** is omitted.)

2. In Unit 17 we mentioned that to form comparatives such *as "bigger than",* the suffix **"-gwo"** is added to the adjective.

   B daaihgwo A.

   B is bigger than A.

   To express adjectives such as *"bigger"* , *"more expensive, "* or *"much bigger, "* **"dī"** or **"hóudō"** is added to the adjective.

   daaihdī ge fóng

   a bigger room

   gwaidī ge fóng

   a more expensive room

   daaih hóudō

   much bigger

   syùfuhk hóudō

   much more comfortable

TRANSLATION

住酒店　　Jyuh Jáudim

訂房

A.　你好，假日酒店。

B.　唔該，我訂一個單人房，住三晚。

A.　好，請問邊日到呢？

B.　星期六下晝，十八號。
　　請問幾錢一晚？

A.　我哋嘅房從每晚港紙千四起，到兩千一晚。

B.　我要間最平嘅就得啦！

A.　O.K. 請問貴姓？

B.　我姓李，李華。

A.　請問點樣付款呢？

B.　用 VISA 信用咭。

A.　信用咭號碼。

B.　4018 0212 3697。

A.　失效期。

B.　95年 10月。

A.　得了，李華先生，多謝你。

喺前台

B. 唔該，我訂咗一個單人房，我叫李華。

A. 請填表。

B. 那，填好啦！

A. 唔該，俾個護照嚟睇吓。

好，搞掂啦，你嘅房號係 613，個 Boy 會同你上樓。

B. 唔該。

換房

B. 唔好意思，我想換間大啲嘅房。

A. 對唔住，我哋啲單人房都係一樣大㗎！

要套間啦！套間會大好多，又舒服好多。

B. 會唔會貴好多呀？

A. 唔會。套間一晚係兩千二，貴八百蚊。啱唔啱呀？

B. 冇問題，想舒服就要使多啲錢！要套間啦！

A. 李生，你嘅套間房號係 2133。嗱，比鎖匙你。

Baakfogùngsì Daaih Gáamga

A Department Store Sale

A. **Wai, "Yuh Wàh" baakfo-gùngsì daaih gáamga, ngóhdeih dōu m̀hóu jāpsyù, heui máaihfāan dī pèhng yéh lā.**

Hey, there is a big sale at Yuh Wah department store. Let's not miss it. We can get some good buys.

B. **Dím pèhng faat a?**

How big is the sale?

A. **Sìhjòng baat ńgh jit héi, yáuh pèhng dou sàam jit tīm.**

Women's clothes start at15% off and go to 70% off.

B. **Pèhng yéh móuh hóu yéh. Ngóh nìhngyún máaih gwaidī, kàmdī.**

Cheap clothes are poor quality. I prefer to buy more expensive clothes that last longer.

A. **Ngóh jī juhkyúh wah: yāt**

I know there is a saying, "You get

fān chìhn, yāt fān fo.
Daahnhaih yìhgā jeuksàam
góng sìhhīng, yiu gáhm kàm
jouhmātyéh.

what you pay for," but fashions change quickly, so why bother paying for something that lasts longer?

B. Gám yauh yáuh douhléih bo.
Yàuhkèihsih yìhgā jauhlàih
gwonìhn, yiu sungláih,
jānhaih yiu máaihfāan dī
pèhng yéh.

You are right. Especially right now with the Chinese New Year coming, I need to buy gifts. I'd rather buy things on sale.

A. Móuh cho la. Yātchàih heui
la.

You can't go wrong. Let's go!

B. Néih jī m̀jī, yùhgwó máaihjò
jìhauh m̀jùngyi, dāk m̀dāk
teuiwuhn ga?

Do you know if I can get a refund or exchange in case I buy it and don't like it?

A. Wuhn jauh dāk, teui jauh
m̀dāk. Néih námjàn sìn
máaih jauh dāk la. Hàahng
lá, "Máihjáugāi" a!

You can exchange, but you can't get a refund. If you think it over before you buy it, there won't be a problem. Let's go so we don't miss it.

B. Hóu lā, heui lā.

Fine. Let's go!

VOCABULARY

daaih gáamga	a big sale
M̀hóu jāpsyù!	Let's not miss it!
pèhng yéh	good buys (inexpensive things)
sìhjòng	fashion clothes
baat ńgh jit	15% off
sàam jit	70% off
Pèhng yéh móuh hóu yéh.	Cheap clothes are poor quality.
nìhngyún	prefer
kàmdī	last longer
Yāt fān chìhn, yāt fān fo.	You get what you pay for.
Gám yauh yáuh douhléih bo.	You are right.
yàuhkèihsih	especially
gwonìhn	Chinese New Year
Móuh cho la.	You can't go wrong.

teui	to refund or return
wuhn	exchange
námjàn	think it over
máaih	buy
"Máihjáugāi!"	Don't miss it! (the sale)

SENTENCE PATTERNS

1. **Sìhjòng baat nǵh jit héi.**
   Women's clothes start at 15% off .

2. **Ngóh nìhngyún máaih gwaidī, kàmdī.**
   I prefer to buy more expensive clothes that last longer.

3. **Néih jī m̀jī, yùhgwó máaihjò jìhauh m̀jùngyi, dāk m̀dāk teuiwuhn ga?**
   Do you know if I can get a refund or exchange in case I buy it and don't like it?

4. **Wuhn jauh dāk, teui jauh m̀dāk.**
   You can exchange, but you can't get a refund.

GRAMMAR NOTES

1. If you are interested in discounts and sales, you will have some fun with these grammar notes. To denote a percentage discount the word *"jit"* is used after the number. The Cantonese way of showing discounts requires simple arithmetic. In English we say *"10% off."* In Cantonese we say in effect *"9 for 10"* so *"10% off"* come out as *"gáu jit"* or *9 discount.* Below are some examples:

(9) **gáu jit**	*10% off*
(8) **baat jit**	*20% off*
(7) **chàt jit**	*30% off*
(8.5) **baat ńgh jit**	*15% off*
(9.5) **gáu ńgh jit**	*5% off*

    Sales are a lot of fun. Some of the expressions illustrate how desperate the shop owner is:

    Daaih Gáamga -*Big Sale*

    Daaih Chēut Hyut - Literally *"Big Out Blood"* or *"Bleeding"* (to death)

    Tiu Láu Fo - Literally *"Jump Building Goods"* or *"The prices are so low I will jump out of the building."*

2. **"Dāk"** *(can)* is an auxiliary verb. It can be put before or after the main verb. For example:

    a)   **Ngóh dāk m̀dāk teuiwuhn ga?**

    Can I get a refund or exchange?

b)   **Wuhn jauh dāk, teu jauh m̀dāk.**

You can exchange, but you can't get a refund.

See the grammar notes in Unit 7 for other usages of **"dāk"** and **"dāk m̀dāk."**

TRANSLATION

百貨公司大減價

Baakfogùngsì Daaih Gáamga

A. 喂，裕華公司大減價，我哋都唔好執輸，去買番啲平嘢啦！

B. 點平法？

A. 時裝八五折起，有平到三折添！

B. 平嘢冇好嘢，我寧願買貴啲，揀啲 。

A. 我知俗語話：一分錢一分貨。但而加著衫講時興，要咁揀做乜嘢？

B. 咁，又有道理嘛！尤其是而加就嚟過年要送禮，真係要買番啲平嘢。

A. 冇錯啦！一齊去啦！

B. 你知唔知，如果買咗之後唔鍾意，得唔得退換㗎？

A. 換就得，退就唔得。

你諗眞先買就得啦！

行啦，"米走雞"呀！

B. 好啦，去啦！

UNIT 23

Góngga
Bargaining

A. Tènggóng, néihdeih
Jùnggwokyàhn ge síhchèuhn
máaih yéh hóyíh góngga.
Haih m̀haih jàn ga?

I was told that when you shop in a
Chinese market you can bargain. Is
that true?

B. Haih jauh haih, bātgwo
yùhgwó kéuihdeih gin néih
haih lóuhfàan, jauh m̀wúih
gáamga.

Yes, but if they see that you are a
foreigner, they won't reduce their
price.

A. Dímgáai a?

Why?

B. Yànwaih kéuihdeih
yihngwàih lóuhfàan sáichín
haih "daaihfāsá," yìhché
yauh m̀sìk góngga.

Because they think that all
foreigners are spendthrifts and that
they don't know how to bargain.

A. Gám jauh cho la. Ngóh
máaih yéh hóu sìk hāan chín,
jyūnmùhn wán pèhng yéh

That is wrong. When I shop, I
know how to save money. I always
look for big sales.

máaih.

B. Yúhgwó ngóh haih néih, ngóh jauh heui siháh tùhng kéuihdeih góngga. Néihge Gwóngdùngwá góng dāk gáhm hóu, pa mātyéh bo.

If I were you, I would try to bargain with them. Your Cantonese is so good, you shouldn't worry.

A. Gwojéung, gwojéung. Bātgwo ngóh jùngyi heui lihnjaahpháh ngóhge Góngdùngwá.

Thank you for the compliment. I would like to go and practice my Cantonese.

B. Néih hàahng sīn la. Ngóh paakchè jìhauh làih wán néih lā.

You go first. After I park the car, I will join you.

A. Hóu lā, ngóh hái deuimihn gàan yùh póu dáng néih.

Fine. I will be waiting for you at that fish store across the street.

C. Sìnsàang, máaih yú la. Yàuhséui sehkbàan a! Hóu sàanmáahng ga!

Sir, would you like to buy some fish? These are live grouper. They're very active.

A. Géichìn pouhng a? Ngóh m̀sīk tái gódī Jùnggwok ge soumuhkjih.

How much are they a pound? I can't read Chinese numbers.

C. Lóuhfáan sínsáang, yàuhsèui sehkbàan, sahp yih mān yāt pouhng.

Mr. Lo Fan (foreigner), live grouper is $12.00 a pound.

A. Yáuh móuh gáaucho a.

Are you kidding? That's so

Gáhm gwai ga. Juhng gwaigwo daaih chìukāpsíhchèuhng ge.

expensive. Yours are even more expensive than those in the big supermarkets.

C. Chìukāpsíhchèuhng ge sehkbàan haih séi ge, nīdī haih yàuhsèui ge. Dímtùhng a. Hóu la, gin néihge Gwóngdùngwá góng dāk gáhm hóu, pèhng yāt mān lā.

Groupers in supermarkets are dead. These are alive. How can you compare them? Because you speak such good Cantonese, I will reduce them a dollar.

A. Mātyéhwá? Pèhng yāt man? Pèhng yātbun la. Luhk mān yāt pouhng la.

What? Only one dollar? How about half price to $6.00?

C. M̀dāk, m̀dāk! Ngóh sihtbún la. Ngóh bòng néih tòngmàaih, pèhng léuhng mān lā.

Impossible! Impossible! I would lose money. I will prepare the fish for you and reduce the price by $2.00.

A. Ngóh móuh daai gáhm dò chín. Luhk mān yāt pouhng ngóh jauh máaih, m̀dāk ngóh jauh jáuh ga la. Bāaibaai.

I didn't bring enough money. If it were $6.00, I would buy it, but if it's more, I will go.

C. Sìnsàang, sìnsàang! Fàanjyuntàuh la! Maaih béi néih la! Luhk mān yāt pouhng.

Sir, sir! Come back, please! I'll sell it to you at $6.00 a pound.

B. Wai, góng hóu ga meih a?

How's the bargaining going?

A. Góng hóu la. Luhk man yāt pouhng, pèhngjó yātbun la.

It's done. $6.00 a pound. Half price!

B. Sòhgwái, bīndouh yáuh pèhng a? Néih tái, "Luhk mān yāt pouhng" sé hái go páai seuhmihn.

You fool! You did not get it any cheaper. Look, $6.00 a pound is written on the sign.

A. Ngāam lā, júngsyun kéuih móuh ngāak ngóh. Ngóh tàamdākyi lihnjaahpháh góngga jē. M̀máaih la! M̀hóuyisi.

That's right. He did not cheat me, though. I was just practicing my bargaining in Cantonese for fun. I'm not going to buy it now. Sorry!

VOCABULARY

tènggóng	I was told
síhchèuhn	market
góngga	bargain
Haih m̀haih jàn ga?	Is that true?
gáamga	reduce (price)
dímgáai	why

yánwaih	because
yihngwàih	think
daaihfāsá	spendthrift
yìhché	besides
cho	wrong
hāan chín	save money
jyūnmùhn	always
si	try
pa	worry; afraid
lihnjaahp	practice
paakchè	park the car
jìhhauh	after
wán	look for
yùh póu	fish store
yàuhséui	live (also: to swim)
sehkbàan	grouper or garoupa

sàanmáahng	active
soumuhkjih	numbers
séi	dead
pèhng yāt mān	reduce a dollar
pèhng yātbun	half price
m̀dāk	impossible
sihtbún	lose money
tòng	butcher; prepare (fish, chicken, duck, etc.)
daai	bring along with
fàanjyuntàuh	come back
maaih	sell
sòhgwái	fool
tái	look
sé	written; write
páai	sign
ngāam	right; correct

ngāak   cheat

júngsyun   at least; finally

tàamdākyi   for fun

SENTENCE PATTERNS

1. **Yúhgwó ngóh haih néih, ngóh jauh heui siháh tùhng kéuihdeih góngga.**
   If I were you, I would try to bargain with them

2. **Ngóh jùngyi heui lihnjaahpháh ngóhge Góngdùngwá.**
   I would like to go and practice my Cantonese.

3. **Ngóh paakchè jìhauh làih wán néih la.**
   After I park the car, I will join you.

4. **Néih dī sehkbàan yú juhng gwaigwo daaih chìukāpsíhchèuhng ge.**
   Your groupers are even more expensive than those in the big supermarkets.

5. **Pèhng yāt mān la.**
   I will reduce them a dollar.

6. **Pèhng yātbun lā.**
   How about half price?

7. **M̀dāk, m̀dāk!**
   Impossible! Impossible!

GRAMMAR NOTES

1. The subjunctive mood *("If I were," "should you" etc.)* is expressed in Cantonese by the word *"yùhgwó" (if)*. No changes are made in the verbs.

   a)   **Yùhgwó ngóh <u>haih</u> néih, ngóh heui Hèunggóng jyuh.**

   If I were you, I would go to Hong Kong to live.

   b)   **Yùhgwó kàhmyaht ngóh yáuh sìhgaan, ngóh jauh làihjó néih ngūkkéi la.**

   If I had had time yesterday, I would have come to your home.

   c)   **Yùhgwó néih yáuh mahntàih, chéng mahn ngóh.**

   Should you have any questions, please ask me.

2. **"Jìchihn"** *(before)* and **"jìhauh"** *(after)* can function as either connectives which introduce a clause or prepositions to form a prepositional phrase. Notice that they are placed at the end of the clause or phrase.

   a)   **Ngóh paakchè <u>jìhauh</u>, (ngóh) làih wán néih.**

   ***After** I park the car, I'll look for you.*

   b)   **Kéuih sīk néih <u>jìchìhn</u>, (kéuih) jouh mātyéh sih?**

   ***Before** she knew you, what did she do?*

   c)   **Baat dím jung <u>jìhauh</u>...**

   ***After** eight o'clock...*

d) **Gáau dím jūng jìchìhn...**

Before nine o'clock...

e) **Sei go yuht jìchihn ngóh heuigwo Hèunggóng.**

I went to Hong Kong four months ago.

3. The suffix *háh* after a verb indicates action which lasts only for a short time.

1. **Béi ngóh táiháh.**

Let me have a look.

2. **Dáng ngóh tùhng kéuih kèngháh.**

Let me talk with him for a while.

3. **Ngóh séung lihnjaahpháh Gwóngdùngwá.**

I wang to practice Cantonese for a while.

TRANSLATION

講價   Góngga

A. 聽講，你哋中國人嘅市場買嘢有價講，係唔係眞㗎？

B. 係就係，不過，如果佢地見你係老番，就唔會減價。

A. 點解呀？

B. 因爲佢哋認爲老番使錢係 " 大花洒 " ，而且又唔識講價。

A. 咁就錯啦！我買嘢好識慳錢，專門搵平嘢買㗎。

B. 如果我係你，就去試下同佢地講價。你啲廣東話講得咁好，怕乜嘢嘛！

A. 過獎，過獎。不過我鍾意去練下我啲廣東話。

B. 你行先啦，我泊車之後來搵你啦！

A. 好啦，我喺對面間魚舖等你。

C. 先生，買魚啦，游水石班魚，好生猛㗎！

A. 幾錢磅呀？我唔識睇嗰啲中國嘅數目字！

C. 老番先生，游水石班，十二蚊一磅。

A. 有冇搞錯呀？咁貴㗎！

重貴過大超級市場。

C. 超級市場嘅石班係死嘅，呢啲系游水嘅點同呀！好啦，見你嘅廣東話講得咁好，平一蚊啦！

A. 乜嘢話？平一蚊？平一半啦！六蚊一磅啦！

B. 唔得，唔得，我蝕本啦！我幫你劏埋，平兩蚊啦！

A. 我冇帶咁多錢，六蚊一磅我就買，唔得我就走㗎啦！

拜拜！

C. 先生，先生，番轉頭啦，賣比你啦，六蚊一磅！

B. 喂，講好價未呀？

A. 講好啦！六蚊一磅，平咗一半啦！

B. 傻鬼，邊度有平呀？你睇，六蚊一磅，寫喺個牌上面！

A. 啱啦，總算佢冇呃我。

我貪得意練下講價啫。唔買啦，唔好意思！拜拜！

LET'S TALK CANTONESE

EMERGENCY AND USEFUL EXPRESSIONS

LET'S TALK CANTONESE

Ṁgòi, je je!	Excuse me, (to get by) please!
Gánghaih lā! Dòngyìhn lā!	Of course!
Ṁsái jáau la!	Keep the change!
Chèuih bín lā!	It's up to you!
Gáaudihm la!	All set!
Yáuh lohk!	Please let me off ! (to a bus driver)
Ṁhóu chòuh lā!	Shut up!
Ṁgòi, sai sāng dī lā!	Can you hold it down a little?
Móuh cho la!	It's right!
Faisih la!	Too much trouble. I'm not going to do it!
Baih la!	It's too bad!
Jàn haih hòisàm.	I'm very happy.
Ṁhóu nàu lā!	Don't be angry!
Ṁsái gam gánjèung!	Take it easy!
Maahnmáan làih lā!	Take your time!

Faaidī lā!	Hurry up!
Hóu tung a!	It hurts!
Néih yáuh móuh sih a?	Are you all right?
Ngóh m̀syùfuhk.	I'm sick.
Néih hó m̀hóyíh sung ngóh heui yīyún a?	Can you send me to the hospital?

*   *   *

Ngóh ga chè séifó la!	The engine of my car has stopped!
Séi lo!	Alas!
Baihgāfó la!	Gosh! O, dear me!
Ngóh ga chè baautāai la!	I have a flat tire.

*   *   *

Gaumehng a!	Help! Help!
Yáuh yàhn chéungyéh a!	Someone has robbed me! Help!
Jùk chahk a!	Stop thief!
Néih jouh mātyéh a?	What the hell are you doing?
Hàahng hòi lā!	Go away!

Ṁgòi, bòng ngóh dá gáu-gáu-gáu bougíng!

Please help me to call 999 to report an emergency!

Ṁhóu gám lā!

Don't do that!

Ṁsài gēng

Don't be scared!

Ṁhóu yūk! Ṁjéun yūk!

Don't move!

Tái jyuh!

Watch out!

Hóu ngàihhím a!

It's dangerous!

Néih chìsin àh?!

Are you crazy?

GLOSSARY

agō	elder brother	亞哥
báau	full	飽
bābai	demanding	巴閉
bākfōng	Northern	北方
Bākgìng choi	Beijing cuisine	北京菜
bāsí	bus	巴士
bāt	pen	筆
bātgwo	but	不過
bātgwo	however	不過
bātyìh	had better	不而
bàhbā	father	爸爸
Bàlàih	Paris	巴黎
baahkcheuhà	poached shrimp	白灼蝦
baahkjáaumgài	boiled chicken	白斬雞
baakfogùngsì	department store	百貨公司
baat dím gáu go jih	a quarter to nine	八點九個字
baat ńgh jit	15% off	八五折

béi	give	比
béi	to	比
bējáu	beer	啤酒
beisyù	secretary	秘書
bīn	while	邊
bīn yaht	what date	邊日
bīngo	who	邊個
Bīngo chéng dōu yātyeuhng lā.	We'll worry about who pays for it later.	邊個請都一樣！
bīngoge	whose	邊個嘅
bīnsyu; bīndouh	where	邊處 邊度
bīnwái	who	邊位
bíu	form	表
bōsí	boss	波士
bòudihnwájùk	talk on the telephone	煲電話粥
bohng	pound	磅
bougou	report	報告
Būtyìh . . .	How about . . .	不而

bun	half	半
cháang	orange	橙
cháangjāp	orange juice	橙汁
cháau	fried	炒
cháau mihn	chow mein	炒麵
chānchìk	relative	親戚
chàh	tea	茶
chàhlàuh	tea house	茶樓
chàsìubàau	steamed pork bun	叉燒包
Chàthéi	7-Up	七喜
chéng	please	請
chéng	invite	請
chéng dángdáng	hold on	請等等
chéngmahn	May I ask ···	請問
chéng dángyātjahn	hold on	請等一陣
chēungyún	spring roll	春卷
chēutheui	leave (Get out!)	出去

LET'S TALK CANTONESE

chè néih heui	give you a ride	車你去
chìh tòih	front desk	前枱
chìhnbihn	in front of	前便
chìmméng	sign	簽名
chín	money	錢
chìngfū	address (you)	稱呼
chìukāpsíhchèuhng	supermarket	超級市場
cho	wrong	錯
chóh	have a seat	坐
choi	dish	菜
chùhng	from	從
chùhng . . . dou	from . . . to	從⋯到⋯
chùng	to prepare (coffee, tea, etc.)	冲
dálàih	call	打嚟
dáng	let	等
dá dihnwá	called	打電話
dàihdái	younger brother	弟弟

dāanyàhnfóng	single room	單人房
dākhàahn	available	得閑
daahngòu	cake	蛋糕
daai	bring along with	帶
daaih gáamga	a big sale	大減價
daaihfāsá	spendthrift	大花洒
Daaihgà dōu gám wah lā.	Wishing you the same.	大家都咁話啦！
daaihhah	building	大廈
Daaihluhk yàhn	Mainland Chinese	大陸人
daap	take	搭
daap chè	take the bus	搭車
dehng fóng	booking a room	訂房
deihtit	subway	地鐵
Deuim̀jyuh!	Sorry!	對唔住！
deuimihn	across from	對面
dī	some	啲
dihnwá	telephone	電話

dihnyíngyún	movie theater	電影院
dīksí	cab	的士
dím-sàm	dim sum	點心
dímgáai	why	點解
dímyéung	how	點樣
dōsou	most of the time	多數
dōu	all	都
dòdī	more	多啲
Dòjeh!	Thank you (for gift).	多謝！
dòsí	toast	多士
dou	to	到
douh	degree	度
dūngtìn	winter	冬天
fán	rice noodle	粉
fàanjyuntàuh	come back	番轉頭
faailohk	happy	快樂
fèigèi	airplane	飛機

fógei	waiter	伙記
fóng	room	房
fòngbihn	convenient	方便
fòngheung	direction	方向
fūkjaahp	complicated	復雜
fùnjùng	minute	分鐘
fuhfún, béichín	pay	付款 比錢
fuhkahn	nearby	附近
fuhnjáau	chicken feet	鳳爪
gáamga	reduce (price)	減價
Gáaudihm.	You're all set.	搞惦
gáhm yiht	this hot	咁熱
gám	in that case	咁
Gám yauh yáuh douhleíh bo.	You are right.	咁又有道理嘛！
Gáulùhng	Kowloon	九龍
gā	with	加

gāai	street	街
gāaiháu	block	街口
gāaisíh	market	街市
gājē	elder sister	家姊
gàmmáahn	tonight	今晚
gàmyaht	today	今日
gàn ngóh làih	follow me	跟我嚟
gafē	coffee	咖啡
gam	so	咁
gau	enough	夠
gau jūng sāugùng	quitting time	夠鍾收工
gauh	piece	嚿
gauhnín	last year	舊年
gayaht	holiday	假日
géi būi	how many cups	幾杯
géi chín	how much	幾錢
Géi hóu, yáuhsàm.	Fine. Thanks!	幾好，有心。

géi, hóu	very	幾；好
Géidākyi bo.	Oh, that's interesting.	幾得意嘞！
géidím	what time	幾點
géidímjūng	when	幾點鍾
géisí, géisìh	when	幾時
géiwái	how many (people)	幾位
gèichèuhng	airport	機場
gihhōng	health	健康
gin yàhnhaak	meet clients	見人客
gìngléih	manager	經理
giu gnóh jouh	call me . . .	叫我做…
gódouh	there	嗰度
góng	say	講
góng	speak	講
góngga	bargain	講價
gónggán	is talking	講緊
gówái	that	嗰位

Gònbùi!	Cheers! Bottoms up!	乾杯！
gòncháau ngàuhhó	fried rice noodles with beef	乾炒牛河
goihgwokyàhn;	foreigner	外國人
fàangwáilóu;	foreigner	番鬼佬
lóuhfàan	foreigner	老番
gùngjok	work	工作
Gùngbóugāidìng	Kung Pao chicken	宮保雞丁
Gùnghéi faatchòih!	Happy Chinese New Year (I wish you good fortune).	恭喜發財！
Gùnghéi!	Congratulations!	恭喜！
gùngsì	company	公司
gùngsihbāau	briefcase	公事包
gùngyún	park	公園
guhngdouh daaihhah	condominium	共渡大廈
gwai	expensive	貴
gwai sing	last name	貴姓
gwaihmín	counter	櫃面

gwaihtúng	drawer	櫃桶
gwójeung	jam	果醬
Gwóngdùng choi	Cantonese cuisine	廣東菜
Gwóngdùngwá	Cantonese	廣東話
gwojéung	to compliment	過獎
gwonìhn	Chinese New Year	過年
hái	at	喺
hái bīndouh	where	喺邊道
hái seuhngmihn, hái seuhngbihn	on top of	喺上面 喺上便
hāan chín	save money	慳錢
hàahng	walk	行
hàahng gùngsì	window shopping	行公司
hàgáau	steamed shrimp dumpling	蝦餃
Hàhng sàng ngàhnhòhng	Hang Seng Bank.	恆生銀行
hahchi	next time	下次
hahgo láihbaaihyaht	next Sunday	下個禮拜日

hahjau	p.m.	下晝
hahptùhng	contract	合同
haih	am, are,is	係
Haih m̀haih jàn ga?	Is that true?	係唔係眞㗎？
Haih mē?	Is that so?	系咩？
hauhbihn	behind	後便
Hèunggóng	Hong Kong	香港
hèungpín	jasmine tea	香片
heui	go	去
heui máaihyéh	go shopping	去買嘢
heuijó	went	去咗
heung chìhn hàahng	walk down	向前行
Hóháu-hólohk	Coca-Cola	可口可樂
hóu	very	好
hóu mòhng	very busy	好忙
Hóu wah la.	Thank you for saying that.	好話啦！
hóuchíh	seem	好似

hóusíu	seldom	好少
hóudō	much more	好多
hòhngbāan	flight	航班
hòi mùhn	open	開門
houh	number	號
houhmáh	number	號碼
hùhngjáu	red wine	紅酒
jáaufàan	give change	找番
jáausou	pay the cashier	找數
jái	son	仔
jáinéui	children	仔女
jáu	wine	酒
jáu	leave	走
jáudim	hotel	酒店
jáujihk	banquet	酒席
jàm	pour	斟
jàn haih	really	眞係
jaahm	station	站

jeui pèhng	cheapest	最平
jeui yiht	hottest	最熱
jí	only	只
jihgēi	myself	自己
jìhhauh	after	之後
jihkdaaht	direct	直達
jīkhaih	mean	即係
jìng	steam	蒸
jip	meet	接
jìujóu, seuhjau	a.m.	朝早，上畫
jóbihn	on the left	左邊
jóuchāan	breakfast	早餐
Jóusàhn!	Good morning!	早晨
Jóutáu!	Good night!	早啲！
joi dá làih	call back	再打嚟
Joigin! Bāaibaai!	Good-bye! Bye-bye!	再見！
		拜拜！
jouh	do	做

jouhsih	work	做事
júngsou	total	總數
júngsyun	at least	總算
jūk	wish	祝
Jūk néih seuhnfùng!	Have a good flight!	祝你順風！
jùngchāangún	Chinese restaurant	中餐館
jùnggwokyàhn	Chinese	中國人
tòhngyàhn	Chinese	唐人
jùngngh	noon	中午
jùngyi	like	鍾意
juhng	still;yet	重
juhng	even	重
Juhng yiu dī mātyéh?	Anything else?	重要啲乜嘢？
jyún	turn	轉
jyún chè	change buses	轉車
jyūnmùhn	always	專門
jyuh	live; stay at	住

kāatpín	business card	咭片
kàhmmáahn	yesterday evening	噚晚
kàhmyaht	yesterday	噚日
kàmdī	last longer	拎啲
kéuih	he, she	佢
kìng	discuss	傾
láahng	cold	冷
láihbaai géi	what day	禮拜幾
láihbaaihyaht	Sunday	禮拜日
láihmaht	gift	禮物
láihbaaisei	Thursday	禮拜四
láihbaaiyih	Tuesday	禮拜二
Laihsih dauhlàih!	Give me "laisih," please!	利是逗嚟！
léuhng	two	兩
léuhng gauh	two pieces	兩嚿
léuihbihn, léuihmihn	inside	裡便
		裡面

lèuhngdī	cooler	涼啲
leng	nice, beautiful	靚
leng	pretty	靚
leuhtsī	lawyer	律師
líhngdou	leader	領導
lihnjaahp	practice	練習
ló	get, bring, fetch	攞
lóuhbáan	boss	老闆
lóuhgùng	husband (slang)	老公
lóuhpòh	wife (slang)	老婆
lóuhsai	boss	老細
lohkchè	get off (bus or train); get out of (car or taxi)	落車
lohksyut	snow	落雪
lohkyúh	rain	落雨
M̀ hóu jāpsyù!	Let's not miss it!	唔好執輸
m̀haih hóu jùngyi	don't like it too much	唔係好鍾意
m̀sái	not necessary	唔使

LET'S TALK CANTONESE

m̀dāk	impossible	唔得
m̀haih	am not, is not, are not	唔係
m̀heui	refuse to go	唔去
m̀jī	don't know	唔知
m̀láahng m̀yiht	mild (not cold, not hot)	唔冷唔熱
m̀sái fàangùng	don't have to go to work	唔使返工
m̀wúih	not really	唔會
m̀yiu	don't want	唔要
máahn	night	晚
máahnhāak	in the evening	晚黑
máaih	buy	買
máaihsung	shop for groceries	買餸
máhfàahnsaai	trouble	麻煩晒
Máihjáugāi!	Don't miss it!	米走雞！
māmìh	mother	媽咪
mān, ngàhnchín	dollar	蚊，銀錢

mātyéh	what	乜嘢
Mātyéh wá?	What?	乜嘢話
Màaihdāan.	Bring me the bill.	埋單
Màhmádéi ! **Gwodākheui.**	So-so.	麻麻哋 ！過得去。
màhmā	mother	媽媽
maahn	slowly	慢
Maahnsih yùhyi!	Hoping all your wishes come true.	萬事如意 ！
maaih	sell	賣
maaihsaai	sold out	賣晒
mahnháh	ask	問吓
mahnhauh	give regards	問候
mahntàih	problem	問題
méihgwok	American	美國
meihgitfān	not married	未結婚
M̀gan yiu!	That's okay.	唔緊要 ！
mihn	noodle	麵

mihnbāau	bread	麵包
móuh	don't	冇
Móuh cho la.	You can't go wrong.	冇錯啦！
móuh jouhyéh	doesn't work	冇做嘢
Móuh mahntàih!	No problem!	冇問題
Móuhdāk-tàahn!	Perfect!	冇得彈！
mònggwó	mango	芒果
M̀sáigāp.	No need to hurry.	唔使急
múi	per	每
mùihmúi	younger sister	妹妹
mùhnháu	door	門口
M̀ gòi! M̀ gòisaai!	Thank you (for service).	唔該！ 唔該晒！
M̀ haih gwa!	No kidding!	唔係呱
M̀ hóuyisi!	Sorry (for embarassment).	唔好意思！
M̀ sái gam haakhei	no need	唔使咁客氣
M̀ sái gam haakhei	You don't have to do	唔使咁客氣啦！

la.	that.	
Ṁ sái la.	That's not necessary.	唔使啦！
Ṁ sáiṁgòi!	Don't mention it.	唔使唔該！
Ṁ saai haakhei!	You're welcome!	唔使客氣
námjàn	think it over	惗眞
nàahm pàhngyáuh	boyfriend	男朋友
ndouh haih	here is	呢道係
néih	you	你
Néih hóu ma?	How are you?	你好嗎？
Néih nē?	And how are you?	你呢？
néui	daughter	女
néuijái	girl	女仔
ngāak	cheat	詭
ngāam	right; correct	啱
ngàhnhòhng	bank	銀行
ngàuhyàuh	butter	牛油
ngàuhyuhk	beef	牛肉
ngàuyuhkyún	beef ball	牛肉丸

ngaanjau	lunch	晏晝
ngóh	I	我
Ngóh chéng néih.	It's my treat.	我請你。
Ngóh jàn haih "mùhng chàh chàh!"	I didn't know about that.	我真係蒙查查！
ngóhdeih	we	我哋
ngóhge	my	我嘅
ngoihbihn	outside	外便
ngūkkéi	family, home	屋企
nīdouh	here	呢喥
nīdouh haih	here is	呢道係
nīhngmùng	lemon	檸檬
nìhngyún	prefer	寧願
pa	worry; afraid	怕
páai	sign	牌
pātìh	party	派對
paakchè	park the car	泊車
pèhng yāt mān	reduce a dollar	減一蚊

pèhng yātbun	half price	半一平
pèhng yéh	good buys (inexpensive things)	平嘢
Pèhng yéh móuh hóu yéh.	Cheap clothes are poor quality.	平嘢冇好嘢
pìhnggwó	apple	蘋果
pòuhtàihjí	grape	葡提子
sái	spend (money)	洗
sāan mùhn	close	閂門
sāanggwó	fruit	生果
sāiyàhn	westerner	西人
sākchè	traffic jam	塞車
sāthaauh	expiration	失效
sàam jit	70% off	三折
sàangyaht	birthday	生日
sàangyi	business	生意
sàanmáahng	active	生猛
sàigwà	watermelon	西瓜

sàilàahnfà	broccoli	西蘭花
sàn	new	新
sàn nìhn	new year	新年
Sànkèihsih cháang	Sunkist orange	新奇士橙
sàntái	body	身體
saanbouh	walk	散步
saigaai	world	世界
sé	written; write	寫
séi	dead	死
séjihlàuh	office	寫字樓
séung	want	想
sèungyàhn	businessman	商人
sehkbāan	garoupa, grouper	石班
sei sahp yih houh bāsí	#42 bus	四十二號巴士
seigwai	four seasons	四季
seuhng chè	get in	上車
seunyuhngkāat	credit card	信用卡

si	try	試
síh jùngsàm	downtown	市中心
síhchèuhn	market	市場
sìhjòng	women's clothes, fashion clothes	時裝
sihk	eat	食
sihkfaahn	have dinner or lunch	食飯
sìhsìh	often	時時
sihtbún	lose money	蝕本
sīk	can	識
sīk louh	know the way	識路
sīn	first; in advance	先
sìngkèinhnǵh, laihbaainǵh	Friday	星期五 禮拜五
sìnsàang	Mr.	先生
sipsih	Centigrade	攝氏
síu sing	last name (humble way)	小姓

síu síu	little	少少
síujé	miss	小姐
sìumáai	steamed barbequed pork dumpling	燒賣
síusihk	snacks	小食
sósìh	key	鎖匙
sòhgwái	fool	傻鬼
soumuhkjih	numbers	數目字
sung	course	餸
syùfuhk	comfortable	舒服
syùnlaaht	sour and hot	酸辣
tái	look	睇
táidábō	ballgame	睇打波
táidihnsih	watch TV	睇電視
táidihnyíng	go to a movie	睇電影
táisyù	read (book)	睇書
tàamdākyi	for fun	貪得意
taaitáai	wife, Mrs.	太太

taam	visit (people)	探
tèng dihnwá	answer the phone	聽電話
tèng gō	a show	聽歌
tènggóng	I was told	聽講
teui	to refund or return	退
tìhm	sweet	甜
tìhn	fill out	填
tìngyaht	tomorrow	聽日
tìnhei	weather	天氣
tīpsī	tip	貼士
tói	table; desk	枱
Tòihwāan yàhn	Taiwanese	台灣人
tòng	soup	湯
tòng	butcher; prepare (fish, chicken, duck, etc.)	劏
tougàan	suite	套間
tūngsèuhng	usually	通常
tùhng	and; with	同

wái	hello (on telephone)	喂！
wán	look for	搵
wàhsih	Fahrenheit	華氏
waahkjé	or (in statement)	或者
dihnghaih	or (in question)	定係
wah	tell	話
wah	say	話
Wah!	Whew!	嘩
Wai!	Hey!	喂
wòtip	potsticker	鍋貼
wúih	will	會
wuhjiu	passport	護照
wuhn	exchange; switch	換
wuihaaksāt	conference room	會客室
yám	drink	飲
yám chàh	have some tea	飲茶
yánwaih	because	因為
yáuh	have	有

yáuh fùng	windy	有風
yáuh gāpsih	in a hurry	有急事
Yáuh mātyéh sih chéng wahdài lá.	Can I take a message?	有乜嘢事請話低啦！
Yáuh mātyeh sih a?	What's going on?	有乜嘢事呀？
Yáuh móuh gáaucho a.	You're kidding!	有冇搞錯！
yáuhsìh	sometimes	有時
yàhn	person	人
yāt baak	one hundred	一百
yāt dā	a dozen	一打
Yāt fān chìhn, yāt fān fo.	You get what you pay for.	一分錢，一分貨。
yāt máahn;	each night; per night	一晚；
múi máahn		每晚
yāt yéung yāt lùhng	one of each	一樣一籠
yātchàih, yātchái	let's	一齊
Yātchai jauh gáaudihmsaai la.	You have almost everything.	一切就搞惦晒！

yātguhng hahmbaahnglaahng	all together	一共 冚唪呤
yātjihk	straight	一直
yātyeuhng daaih	same size	一樣大
yàuhgúk	post office	郵局
yàuhkèihsih	especially	尤其是
yàuhséui	live (also: to swim)	游水
yahplàih	come in	入嚟
yaht kèih	date	日期
yauh haih	also	又係
yauhbihn	on the right	右便
yèuhng hóng	foreign company	洋行
yìhnhauh	then	然後
yìhché	besides	而且
yìhgā	now	而加
yihngwàih	think	認爲
yihnsīk	to know each other	認識
yiht	hot	熱

yihtgwo	hotter than	熱過
Yìnggwok yàhn	British	英國人
yiu	want	要
yiu hòiwúi	have a meeting	要開會
yú	fish	魚
yúhn	far	遠
yùh póu	fish store	魚舖
yùhgwó	if	如果
yuht	month	月

NOTES

NOTES

NOTES

NOTES